LYRICS

BY THE LETTER H.

(Chs. Grahame Halpine)
1829-1868

NEW-YORK:
J. C. DERBY, 8 PARK PLACE.
CINCINNATI:
H. W. DERBY.
1854.

Printed by HOLMAN, GRAY & CO., N. Y.

TO

CHARLES GORDON GREENE,

OF THE BOSTON POST,

A TRUE MAN AND GOOD FRIEND,

This Volume is Inscribed.

CONTENTS.

	Page.
THE CHEMISETTE,	7
TIME,	9
THE BALL-ROOM BELLE,	11
LABOR'S WAR SONG,	13
A HYMN TO THE TYPES,	17
THE FERRY-BOATS OF GOTHAM,	23
TO AZRA,	25
AN EXILE'S GRAVE,	30
PASSION,	34
FORGIVE,	37
THE OLD YEAR AND THE NEW,	38
THE HOUSEHOLD TOMB,	42
"A DOLLAR IN HIS POUCH,"	45
THE LIFE CHASE,	47
GAGE D'AMOUR,	49
A WINTER LYRIC,	52
THE MYSTIC VOICE,	55
THE MIDNIGHT WATCH,	58
TO LAURA,	60
THE MOURNERS,	62
THE STARS OF MEMORY,	66
A COLLEGE SONG,	70
THE RUBY,	72
THE CHALLENGE CUP,	75
WEBSTER,	77
MORE LIGHT,	78
ITALIAN FREEDOM,	80
A RUSHING MELODY,	82
THE RHYMER'S RITUAL,	87
A BROADWAY BELLE,	90
A VERY TENDER BALLAD,	92
THE NYMPH OF LURLEIBERGH,	104
A WINDY DISSERTATION,	107
THE OLD BACHELOR'S NEW YEAR,	111
SOME WISDOM IN DOGGEREL,	113
THE OPIUM DREAM,	115
WIDOWOLOGY PHILOSOPHIZED,	117
THE WELL-DRESSED MAN,	119
WOMAN'S RIGHTS,	121
THE ISLANDS THAT AWAIT US,	124

PAGE.
A CALIFORNIAN DITTY, ... 127
IGDRASIL, ... 130
THE BACHELOR'S ADIEU, ... 132
THE CRYSTAL PALACE, ... 136
THE MORNING SERENADE, ... 140
ROMANCE AND ECHO, ... 142
FLEUVE DU TAGE, ... 144
WHY LOVE THE TURK AND HATE THE CZAR, . . . 145
DUET FOR THE BREAKFAST TABLE, ... 151
THE PRISONER OF WAR, ... 154
MATRIMONIAL COMPLACENCY, ... 157
WE MIGHT HAVE BEEN, ... 159
SOME TALK ABOUT POETS, ... 160
THE LAST MOSQUITO, ... 162
SPIRIT RAPPING, ... 165
THE BROKEN HEART, ... 167
THE FIRST OF MAY, ... 168
THE LAST RESORT, ... 170
THINE EYES OF BLUE, ... 171
THE THRONE AND THE WORKSHOP, ... 172
THE LAST APPEAL, ... 174
A PUNGENT CONSIDERATION, ... 175
NEW-YORK CRYSTAL PALACE, ... 179
TRUTH IN PARENTHESIS, ... 185
ORIGIN OF THE HAIR CHAIN, ... 187
MAXIMS OF THE NEWSPAPERS, ... 189
ADIEU, ... 191
THE CRUSADER SONG, ... 192
SONNETS, ... 195
THE BACCHANTE, ... 200
THE MINER'S DREAM, ... 201
ALAS! THEY MET, ... 202
FEMININE ARITHMETIC, ... 203
ROMEO AND JULIET, ... 204
THE MUSHROOM HUNT, ... 207
THE TURQUOIS, ... 208
LINES, ... 209
A MAINE-LAW LYRIC, ... 211
A PALPABLE PARODY, ... 214
AN OLFACTORY ODE IN PRAISE OF NEW-YORK CLEANLINESS, 215
RIME OF YE SEEDIE PRINTEERE MAN, ... 218
A TEMPERANCE PARODY 221
THE LOST CITY BROOM, ... 223
EPIGRAM, ... 228

Lyrics by the Letter H.

THE CHEMISETTE.

O Chemisette! the fairest yet
   That e'er hid bosom purer, whiter!
Thou dost not know what envious woe
   Thy veiling snow hath given the writer.
So trimly frilled—so plumply filled!
   And then the eyes that shine above it!
I burn—I long—nor is it wrong,
   (At least in song,) dear girl, to love it.

Sweet Chemisette! the coral set
   To chain thy folds in gentle duty,
Flings round a glow upon the snow
   To heighten so thy blushing beauty:
And ne'er before, on sea or shore,
   Did coral feel a softer billow—
Nor could the gold around it rolled,
   Though ten times told, deserve the pillow!

O Chemisette! below thee met
  A rosy ribbon binds her bodice:
And in her mien is clearly seen
  One half the queen, and one the goddess.
Her voice is low—how sweet its flow!
  Her upper lip disdains the under:
Her curls are like dark waves that strike
  A marble cliff—then rush asunder.

O ripening grace! O radiant face!
  When love is love it knows no measure!
Her hands are small, but yet can call
  The power of music at their pleasure:
And as they peep from sleeves of deep,
  White Brussell's lace, "La mode Ramillies,"
Her fingers seem, or else I dream,
  Like stamens in the bells of lilies.

As clouds of spring on feathery wing
  Obscure the blushing heaven a minute,
So, Chemisette! thy silvery net
  Now veils the heaven that glows within it.

Oh, bear me up! I faint, I droop,
My glowing pulses throb and tingle—
Immortal bliss! but grant me this,
In such a Heaven one hour to mingle!

TIME.

I.

Time rolls away, and bears along
A mingled mass of right and wrong;
The flowers of love that bloomed beside
The margin of its summer tide;
The poison-weeds of passion, torn
From dripping banks, and headlong borne
Into that unhorizoned sea
Which mortals call eternity.

II.

Noiseless and rapid as a dream,
For ever flows the widening stream;
While every wave, or transient hour,
Heaves up a weed and takes a flower.

The isle of life, that seemed to be
A continent infinity,
Grows bleaker, narrower, day by day,
And channelled by a salter spray.

III.

Like shipwrecked men who closelier flock
To the bare summit of the rock,
When the loud storm that wrecked them flings
A loftier billow from its wings,—
We climb from youth's wave-rippled strand
With heavier heart and feebler hand
Up the gray rock of age, whose peak
Time's mounting billows surge and seek.

IV.

There from the barren top espy
A girth of tears,—an ashen sky;
Bowed heads, cold hearts and palsied feet
To age's pinnacle retreat;
While the dull tide that swells below
Pursues them with a sullen flow:
The rock is hid,—the waves beat high—
And, lo!—an ocean and a sky!

THE BALL-ROOM BELLE.

She wore a satin slipper
  A pair of silvery shoon,
And seemed the daintiest tripper
  In all the gay saloon—
Her robe of pink was covered
  With richest Limerick lace:
And sweet good-humor hovered
  Around her dimpling face.

Her hair was brown, or golden,—
  It changed as fell the light—
Her bodice scarce could hold in
  Her bosom's heaving white:
Her eyes were gay and merry
  As a fountain in the shade,
And her voice was sweet and cheery
  As the thoughts that it conveyed.

She bent as may the lily
  When the morning-breezes glide
Adown the upland hilly
  To the river's rippling side;

She waltzed, and, as outfloating
  Her robes and ringlets streamed,
I could not keep from noting
  How fairy-like she seemed.

But when with heightened color
  She ceased the whirling dance,
A strange and panting pallor
  Came o'er her countenance,
I asked her—" O, forgive me,—
  Can I serve you ?—nay,—I will—
My fears do not deceive me,
  You are—you must be ill ?"

Then she, with timid glances,
  From lips as sweet as thyme,
Replied—" These eastern dances
  Ill suit our western clime;
Could you—it might relieve me "—
  (I rose upon the hint)—
" A glass of water give me,
  With a glass of—BRANDY IN 'T ?'

LABOR'S WAR SONG.

I.

Up, brethren! up! The world is not
  So bad as some would make it;
Although we till a stubborn lot,
  The plough of toil can break it;
And wheat,—a sea of amber froth,—
  White apple bloom, and blushing cherries,
Will soon replace the thistle growth
  And bitter bramble-berries!—
For life's a field, a goodly field,
  Where skill and long endeavor
Can make the barren wilderness
  An Eden bower for ever!

II.

Wherever Reason bids you go,
  Be firm resolved to follow!
Ne'er build a house on Age's snow—
  Tradition is but hollow.
With eyes that never shun the light,
  Although it show your past mischances,

Ride down the phantom brood of night
  With troops of gallant fancies!
For life's a fight, a stubborn fight,
  Where hope and fresh endeavor
Can overcome the hosts of Care,
  For ever and for ever!

III.

If Anguish hems you in upon
  Some bleak and lonely mountain,
Ne'er sigh for the forsaken lawn,
  And willow-shaded fountain;
But, on the lightning-shivered top,
  Learn of the eagle, self-reliance,
And let the whirlwinds, as they drop,
  Bear down your bold defiance!
For life's a fight, a gallant fight,
  Where heart and strong endeavor
Shall win the palm and wear the palm
  For ever and for ever!

IV.

Besieged in Want's despised retreat,
  With friends and funds but scanty,

Fling over half the bread you eat,
  That men may think you've plenty;
'Twas thus the Goth was driven from Rome;
  And 'tis a maxim broadly Roman,—
Though bitter tears may fall at home,
  Laugh loud before your foeman!
For life's a siege, a long-drawn siege,
  A fierce, protracted trial,
Where fate for ever gives the palm
  To hope and self-denial.

V.

Should those you friended in distress
  Forget you—'tis the fashion—
Ne'er let them know their worthlessness
  Had power to move your passion!
Be cool, and smile—the war of life
  Again may place you far above them;
And, should you chance to meet in strife,
  Then, prove how much you *love* them!
For life's a fight, a varying fight,
  Defeat and victory blended,—
Though Wrong may triumph for awhile,
  Right wins ere all is ended!

VI.

Should she who shared your summer lot,
  Now shun your cold caresses,
Oh, blame her not!—oh, hurt her not!
  But loose her golden jesses;
She never loved,—no power on earth
  Can change a woman's true affection;
Nor is the haggard falcon worth
  A moment's sad dejection.
Forget her frailty in the fight,
  Where brain and bold endeavor,
Still win at will a changeless crown
  For ever and for ever!

VII.

Avoid the fruitless strife of creed—
  You cannot turn nor guide it;
Let Heaven award the victor's meed,
  And Priest with Priest decide it!
Believe that life is fleeting breath,
  Be just to man and love your neighbor,
And take this ritual for your faith,—
  "Truth, Temperance, and Labor!"

And thus the error-clouds that veil
  The heaven of life will sever,
And God's approving eye look down
  On Faith and firm Endeavor.

A HYMN TO THE TYPES.

I.

O silent, myriad army, whose true metal
  Ne'er flinched nor blenched before the despot Wrong!
Ye brethren, linked in an immortal battle
  With time-grown Falsehoods, tyrannous and strong!
Fragments of strength and beauty lying idle,
  Each in its place, until the appointed day,
Then, swift as wheels the squadron to the bridle,
  Ye spring into the long compact array!

II.

Obedient, self-contained and self-contented,
  Like veteran warriors in the mingled broil,
Each giving help where just his help is wanted,
  Nor seeking more than his due share of toil.

Striving, not vainly, each to be a leader,
  Your capitals are captains of the file,
The crown you aim at, to inform the reader,
  And help old Truth on for another mile!

III.

What wondrous dreams of beauty may be flying,
  Unwinged, unuttered, through your silent mass!
Even as a prism in some deep grotto lying,
  Until the informing soul of Genius pass,
Filling the cavern with a light as tender
  As that which breaks from Love's half downcast eyes;
Then the cold gem awakes to rainbow splendor,
  Where, couched in moss, beside the fount it lies.

IV.

Oh! what a burst of glory when ye mingle
  Your bloodless hands in the support of truth!
When to your banded spell the pulses tingle
  Of tottering age and fiery-visioned youth!
What power and strength when ye stand up united
  Beneath the master-spirit's guiding sway!
A thousand lamps at one lone altar lighted,
  Turning the night of error into day!

V.

Ye are the messengers all earth pervading,
   Which speak of comfort and communion still!
Planks of a mighty ship, whose precious lading
   Is man's just reason, and his heart's fond will.
Launched on the stream of time, our thoughts are drifted
   Far, far adown our children-peopled shore,
And the gay pennon of our hope is lifted
   When him it cheered through life it cheers no more!

VI.

Unmarshalled army! earth is still a wonder,
   A bright God's wonder, all too little known!
Star-eyes above us and the green sod under,
   Oceans of beauty girdling every zone!
And man himself, whose deep heart throbs for ever
   With passionate longings, and the fierce unrest
Of hopes that struggle in a vain endeavor
   To hear themselves by other lips confest.

VII.

Ye are the mightier tongues we have invented
   To bear our utterance ever and allwhere,

Our hearts into a thousand hearts transplanted,
  A multiplied existence ye confer !
Falsehood with bloodshot eyes awoke from slumber,
  And glared in baleful terror on your birth,
Meek-fronted Truth enrolled you in her number,
  And cried, " I am not without hope on earth !"

VIII.

Ye are true types of men ! When disunited,
  The world has nothing feebler or more vain !
But, when one animating thought has lighted
  The dim recesses of each heart and brain,
The mass rolls onward with a steady motion,
  Warned by Truth's beacon from the rock of Death,
The breath of Knowledge sweeps the stagnant ocean,
  And men rise up like billows at its breath—

IX.

Rise up and shake the beetling cliffs of error,
  Pour through its hollow base with thund'rous din !
Shake down the columns which have shed a terror
  And a dark shadow round the bay, wherein,

Landlocked in God's deep love, our bark, undamaged,
Shimmers among the countless skiffs that sail
That "bay of life" where heaven and earth are imaged,
And Nature gleams through Passion's liquid veil!

x.

Ye are the swords of Truth—the only weapon
That Truth *should* wield in this protracted war,—
Ye are the rocks of Knowledge that we step on,
In thought's bright firmament, from star to star!
I see an angel winged in every letter,
Even as man's soul is hid within his clay!
I see a prisoner with his broken fetter
Emerging out of darkness into day!

XI.

Unspeakable ye are! We have created
A new existence than our own more firm;
Our life and hopes into your life translated
Enjoy a being that shall know no term!
The ploughman's frolic-song still kindles gladness
Within the heart, though care has gnawn its core,
And bright eyes weep at his recorded sadness
Who sleeps where pride and envy sting no more!

XII.

Even as the marble block contains all beauty,
Enshrined in darkness and the outward husk,
Which the warm sculptor, with love-prompted duty,
Shall make to shine, through darkness and through dusk,
Into the day of loveliness,—ye treasure
All forms of thought and song in your mute sphere,—
Our pen the chisel, and our rhyme the measure
By which we make the *inborn* god appear!

XIII.

Would that my heart were wider-tongued and deeper,
Nor moved involved in cares of meaner place!
Then would I mow down like a sturdy reaper
The crop of thought that rises from the *case.*
Flowers of bright song and fruits of mellow reason,
And many a peeping bud of infant Truth,
My soul should garner in its summer season,
And steep in dews of a perpetual youth!

XIV.

But ah, mute types! are ye not all too often
Constrained to serve at some unsolaced toil?

To harden hearts that ye would love to soften,
  And help to swell where ye would still the broil ?
Even so with me !—my dreams of song are hurried
  Like moon-ray flashes through the drifting storm,
And all that God made noble in me, buried
  In wants I share in common with the worm !

THE FERRY-BOATS OF GOTHAM.

The ferry-boats of Gotham—
  How gloriously they glide,
With lamps of red and lamps of blue
  Across the starless tide !
Through long defiles of blazing light
  On each street-studded shore ;
No sound to break the hush of night,
  Except the paddles' roar.

Around the island city lie,
  Encircling block and mart

Vast ships that rear against the sky
  A forest-growth of art;
And girdled thus with winged might,
  Though now the wings are furled,
Manhattan is what Venice was,
  The Sea-Queen of the world!

O ferry-boats!—the argosies
  That tyrants launched of yore,
To bring them gold, and gems, and spice,
  From India's plundered shore,
Ne'er knew a freight so rich as this,
  That humbly, day by day,
To Brooklyn homes and social ease
  From business ye convey.

Let Russia launch her birds of prey
  Against the Crescent Moon,
And butcher in Sinope's bay
  The convoy of Batoon;
Let France and England, holding back,
  Deny the aid they swore,
Until the Sea that once was Black
  Grows red with Turkish gore;

But ye, undaunted ferry-boats!
  Your pathless course pursue;
Nor any nobler navy floats,
  Nor manned by hearts more true!
Your mission is to spread content,
  Love, joy, and wealth to bear—
Odds-life! I HAVN'T GOT A CENT
  TO PAY MY BLESSED FARE!

TO AZRA.

I.

We meet once more. The early bloom
  Of passion perished in its pride,
And slumbers in a foreign tomb
  Beyond a dark and stormy tide:
The young Evangel faded fast
  From its ethereal form to clay;
The sea of anguish—but 'tis past,
  And we have met once more to-day.

II.

Thy cheek with paler tinge imbued—
  Thine eyes—ah ! where their mirthful glance
A spirit calmed, but not subdued,
  Breathes o'er thy gentle countenance.
Ah me ! how bright, in olden days,
  The smile that played on lip and chin !
But now, as through a setting haze,
  The sun peeps sadly from within.

III.

Thy voice is changed ; no more its tone
  From music's ocean may emerge ;
Thy laugh is mingled with a moan,
  Thy words of hope resound a dirge ;
And ever through thy gay discourse
  Some thread of suffering winds along—
A clue that leads with mystic force
  To the deep fount of sadder song.

IV.

Love lives,—perhaps in purer form,—
  But ah ! its magic thrills no more ;

The ship-wrecked pilgrim of the storm
  May prize his chance-directed shore;
But from its barren cliffs his eye
  Will range in vain the circling seas,
And picture a more brilliant sky,—
  A lovelier land, that once was his.

V.

Thy hand!—time was, its faintest touch,
  Like sacred fire, lit up my frame!
Those dreams of youth—those hours had much
  That memory fondly loves to claim.
I dreamed;—my soul lay soft and hushed
  As was the sod beneath thy feet;
It gave its flowers, and they were crushed—
  And, once again, *once more* we meet.

VI.

Henceforth the world may smoother pass,
  But life's bright star shines cold and dim;
Though fortune prove a sea of glass,
  O'er which our lives uninjured swim,—

Far better were the storm, the strife
  Which overcast our earlier suns!
There is a record kept in life
  Where love but stamps his signet once.

VII.

We meet once more,—Oh, ne'er to part
  While life and power to live remain;
One great wrench of the startled heart,
  And it can feel no second pain.
No second pang can bid me roam,
  Like that first throb too deep to bear,
When, standing in my shattered home,
  I woke from bliss to face despair.

VIII.

And months—aye, long, unsolaced years
  Have found me reckless, loveless, wild—
A man who is not, but appears
  The living jest at which he smiled.
There is a pleasure born of pain,
  When all its outward signs depart,—
A triumph when the steadfast brain
  Floats calmly o'er the struggling heart.

IX.

The lip that quickest wings the jest,
  Is first to breathe the secret sigh;
The laugh that rings with freshest zest
  But chokes the floodgates of the eye;
The heart, like Egypt's Queen of old,
  Ne'er lets its misery see the light;
But o'er the deadly asp we fold
  The garments of the gala night.

X.

Forbear thy early fire to feign,
  Nor weep that I am colder grown;
With less of joy, and less of pain,
  The heart assumes a temperate tone.
Can prayers or tears revive the flowers
  Which glowed and withered, *shrunk*, and died?
Can we recall the golden hours
  Whose waves are in the eternal tide?

XI.

The Hand that wrote the Persian's fall,
"'Weighed, wanting, worthless, cast aside,"—

The dark hand on the glittering wall
 Was but the touchstone to his pride.
Adversity—another hand—
 Revealed thy falsehood, and my fate;
Long years of sorrow, a strange land;
 And restoration,—given TOO LATE!

AN EXILE'S GRAVE.

He sleeps; and o'er his humble grave
No gilded trophy meets the view:
And yet, the man beneath was true,
 Just, resolute and brave.

He paid his folly's furthest debt—
Inurn it with his baser part!
His qualities of mind and heart
 Will long survive him yet.

Who blames a weakness born of woe?
The agony that sought relief
In that which can but deepen grief,
 Is not for them to know.

O friends! it is a bitter thing
To die alone, in a wide land—
Without a friend, without a hand
Or hope or help to bring!

To know our bones may never rest
In the green valleys of our youth,—
To feel that many a foul untruth
Our memory may molest!

He bared against a vengeful foe,
The steel to freedom consecrate;
And died, the victim of a hate
That spares nor high nor low.

For there ARE ways of killing men
Beside the sword, the axe, the rope,—
Great hearts will break when lost to hope,
And yet no blood be seen.

In simplest guise, and borne by some
Who knew his worth—his will to bless—
He presses, as our noblest press,
The couch of Martyrdom.

Last night I dreamed I did attain
The peak of Heaven's crystalline towers,
And there was marshalling of powers
Beneath me on the plain.

In golden suits, with floating plumes,
The Martyr-army gathered fast—
Men who to this bright realm had passed
Out from earth's prison glooms.

Each rode upon a golden car,
His name in brilliants traced thereon;
But brightly as the brilliants shone,
The names were brighter far;

Bright with the glow of Nationhood;
Bright with historic love and truth,
And steeped in the perpetual youth
Of human gratitude!

And gathering fresh accessions still,
With cymbal-clang and bugle-blow,
And pennons fluttering to and fro,
The tide swept down the hill;

Down to that gate, whose ample size
Is studded thick with worlds and stars—
That gate whose azure only bars
This Heaven from earthly eyes.

And there was ONE who entered in,
And bowed in mute submission down:
" Unworthy I to wear the crown—
Unworthy by my sin !"

* * * * * * *

The vision passed ! Let him who ne'er
Hath felt the long-protracted pains,
The life in death of prison chains,
Speak lowly and beware !

Let him who ne'er was gagged and torn
From home and kindred far away—
Who hath not steeped from day to day
His bread in tears of scorn ;

Let him be mute or meekly pray,
Thus kneeling on the sainted sod—
" Thy sore temptations known to God,
Have washed thy sins away !"

PASSION.

Passion suggests its own discourse,
Not checked, nor helped, by rule or form;
It utters by instinctive force
An eloquence, deep, terse and warm.
It is not fanciful, nor strains
For words or thoughts beyond its reach;
The molten fury of the veins
Glows through the lens of crystal speech.

It grasps and crushes into mould
Whate'er can serve its headlong need;
The weapon may be brass or gold,
But it must make the victim bleed!
Imagination's furthest flight
Is harnessed to its arm-ed wheel,
Sunward or hellward—wrong or right—
It will not think,—it can but feel!

'Twas born of Love, and nursed by Hate—
It lives in Sorrow's shattered tower;
Its only creed, a blinded fate—
Its only hope, a shorter hour;

Its only joy, the rugged zest
  With which we hear the whirlwind rave;
Its only friend, a stubborn breast;
  Its only Sabbath, in the grave!

It lives in pain—in fierce desire,
  Or vain regret for perished joy;
Its aspirations have the fire
  Which tortures, but will not destroy!
It is Prometheus bound again
  Amid the elemental strife;
It is the crown and scourge of men—
  The road to death—the fact of life!

Its joys are full luxuriant flowers,
  Though nurtured on a mouldering root;
Though watered by the bitterest showers,
  And bearing a most bitter fruit.
The corpse of Love emits a ray
  Ere yet the electric glow has gone;
The lurid twilight of decay
  Pretends itself a rising dawn!

A star to swift destruction hurled,
  Our planet's changeless orbit crossed;

" Behold! behold a larger world!
   It nears!—it grows—and ah! 'tis lost!"
Thus when man, torn by Passion, flies
   From the calm round of centred thought,
He flashes through the steady skies
   And sinks—reduced, obscured, forgot!

O Passion!—could we turn aside
   Thy diamond-lipped and golden bowl—
Avoid the rich delirious tide
   That poisons while it thrills the soul!
Could woman's peerless form convey
   Its beauty only to the brain,
How many a cheek were dry to-day
   Down which the tides of anguish rain!

It may not be! The inner fire
   Defies reproof's exterior flood;
It is the marrow of the bone—
   The surging current of the blood!
The bosom chords that thrill to sin
   Will thrill until for ever hushed;
The heart that has the worm within
   Must bleed before that worm is crushed!

FORGIVE.

Judge not harshly !—O, remember,
Thou thyself hast need of ruth ;
And let mercy's accents temper
Even the rigid words of truth !
Through a glass with error clouded,
Thou dost all my faults behold,
But the springs are darkly shrouded
Whence the tide of passion rolled.

Think not that I seek to blind you
To my folly, to my shame ;
Think not that I hope to find you
Once deceived, and still the same !
Friendship—hope—love—all are forfeit,
Trampled, shattered, or decayed—
And for passion's deadly surfeit,
Years of anguish must be paid.

Yet I would not that you chase me
From your thoughts, and yet, I would !
May the future ne'er replace me
In the niche where once I stood ?

If my memory e'er be painted,
  Let it wear the shape it wore,
When our souls were first acquainted
  In the happy days of yore!

Fare thee well! my days of pleasure
  Were not worth the sighs they cost;
Yet the heart will sadly measure,
  What is gained, with all it lost!
Madness—pain—for these I bartered
  Love as rich as yours to me;
And the ship with promise chartered,
  Sank in an unclouded sea!

THE OLD YEAR AND THE NEW.

The good Old Year hath run his race,
  And his latest hour draws near;
The cold dew shines on his hoary face,
And he hobbles along with a listless pace,
To his lonely and snow-covered resting-place
  In the northern hemisphere.

See, how his stiff joints faint and shrink,
   As the cold breeze whistles by!
He has a bitter cup to drink,
As he watches the sand in the hourglass sink;
Standing alone on the icy brink
   Of the gulf of eternity!

His scanty robe is wrapped more tight,
   As the dim sun dwindles down:
Not a star arises to cheer the night
Of him whose temple they once made bright,
When crimson roses and lilies white
   Half hid his golden crown.

He reels,—he slips,—no power at hand
   To check him from tumbling o'er!
The hourglass clicks with its latest sand,
Each moment falls like the stroke of a brand
On one already too weak to stand,—
   He falls!—he is seen no more!

And lo!—in the east a star ascends,
   And a burst of music comes!
A young lord, followed by troops of friends,
Down to the broad equator wends,

While the star that travels above him bends
O'er a sea of floating plumes.

And Hope springs up from the couch of Care—
Her eyes are full of the softest fire;
A light burns round her golden hair,
And her bosom is soft, and O, how fair!
As she clasps the boy and presses him there—
As once she pressed his sire!

On every hill the bonfire glows,
And clarions blend with the beating drums;
The yellow crocus disparts the snows,
And the river, freed from its bondage, flows,
While sparrows chirp and the shrill cock crows—
As the New Year hitherward comes!

His glittering mail he flings aside
And we see a robe of the brightest green;
And the velvet-green but serves to hide
The crimson vest of the richer pride,
He dons in the brilliant summer-tide,
When he weds his harvest queen.

But Time rolls on; and the conqueror turns
His wearying feet to the frozen North.
The sun each day more dimly burns,
And the Mother Earth each day inurns
Her summer brood, while the cold wind spurns
The Victor it heralded forth!

And again an Old Year treads alone
To the North, bereft of friends.
He totters along to the frozen zone,
With an icicle in each marrowless bone,
And the hoarse wind buries his dying groan
As another Star ascends.

Then kindly think of the dying year,
The joys, the hopes, and the love he nursed!
Let fall a tear on his narrow bier,
For altho' not perfect, yet much I fear
That he was the best we shall ever see here,—
God grant he may prove the worst!

THE HOUSEHOLD TOMB.

I.

The shafts of disappointment fall
  Where most we build our pride;
And now the dearest loved of all
  Their little ones had died!
The tears they shed in silence fell
  Like raindrops through the gloom—
And unto him they loved so well
  They reared this household tomb!

II.

The little bird, whose tender wing
  Grew weak in winter tide,
Who seemed to strengthen in the spring,
  And soared in summer's pride,—
Grew fainter as the autumn fell
  On summer's withering bloom,
And unto him they loved so well,
  They built this household tomb!

III.

He had a trick in sunny hours
  To seek the garden walks,

And pluck from out the radiant flowers
  The withered buds and stalks;
He bore them in as if to tell
  That canker worms consume,—
And soon to him they loved so well—
  They reared the household tomb!

IV.

The church hath massive iron gates,
  Six days 'tis cold and dim,
Till Sunday fills the silken seats
  And the organ swells the hymn;
Shall there a blazoned pillar tell
  A child's so common doom?
Ah no!—for him they loved so well
  They rear a household tomb!

V.

On the mantelpiece, so old and worn,
  Where his childish toys were laid,
Where the withered buds he plucked were borne,
  In the room where oft he played,—
An angel statue sheds a spell
  Of prayer around the room;

And the angel boy they loved so well
  Has now a household tomb!

VI.

O friend! I've seen the teardrops shine,
  And watched thy quivering lip,
I've felt thy arm clutch closer mine
  When a rosy boy did trip
Across our path; and though there fell
  No tear, nor word of gloom,—
I knew thy spirit knelt before
  That little household tomb!

VII.

But, comfort! There's a higher sphere
  Where the earth-lost reunite!
The spirit of thy boy seems near
  To prompt each word I write:
He says he shares the loved ones' mirth
  When they gather in the room,
And smiles down on the social hearth,
  Even from the household tomb!

"A DOLLAR IN HIS POUCH."

I.

'Tis pleasant when our friends are rich
  To meet them day by day;
Or good, or ill—no matter which—
  Provided they can pay.
But is there one—you answer not—
  Who would, or could avouch
Esteem for one who hadn't got
  A dollar in his pouch?

II.

'Tis pleasant with our friends to dine,
  To see them well arrayed,
To bumper them in costly wine
  For which themselves have paid,
To smoke with them—to drive about—
  Share cup, caress and couch;
But should we know a man without
  A dollar in his pouch?

III.

The bride will love the pleading swain
  Who has at his command

A " brown-stone front," a goodly train
  Of equipage and land.
But should his fortune cease to smile,
  E'en Lore away will slouch—
" Why *can't* the creature show a pile
  Of dollars in his pouch ?"

IV.

On sea, on shore, they seem to say
  " He's rich and can't be dull,"
The gold within his porte-monnaie,
  They think, can fill his skull ;
Let Mammon reign—let Genius rot—
  Let Wit, Lore, Valor crouch !
Poor devils ! Have they any got
  A dollar in his pouch ?

V.

If Christ again should visit earth,
  A man of toil and care,
Howe'er divine—whate'er his worth,
  How think you would he fare ?
" Hence with this vagrant ! thrust him out !
  Some swindler I dare vouch ;
Think you God's son would come without
  A dollar in his pouch ?"

THE LIFE-CHASE.

They started when the morning blushed
Above the wave;
Earth, in its dewy freshness, hushed
As is the grave!
They started, whence a torrent rushed
Down from the hill—
And many a flower their footprints crushed,
On hurrying still.

A rosy child (the quarry) tripped
Adown the vale;
Each dewdrop from the rose he sipped,
And lily pale—
Oft in the limpid stream he dipped
Nor thought of fear;
But merry-eyed, and laughing-lipped,
Made music there.

He recked not that he was pursued,
So youth is blind!
But mocked the dull decrepitude,
That lagged behind—

He sought the covert of a wood,
And loudly laughed!
"Old Huntsman of the fearful mood,
I scorn thy shaft!"

Nor frowned, nor smiled, the huntsman old,
But tottered on;
His eyes were keen, his hands were cold,
His visage wan!
A drapery of darkness rolled
Around his form;
And still he chased through wood and wold,
Through shine and storm!

When evening o'er the mountains came,
The child grew weak;
Gone the rich vigor of his frame,
And pale his cheek!
But the Huntsman's eyes are still aflame
And deep his breath!
Life is that Huntsman's dying game,
That Huntsman, Death!

GAGE D'AMOUR.

A simple rosebud once, as simply given,
And yet it led astray,
In passion's devious way,
Two souls from heaven.

'Twas simply offered—taken without thought;
But images arose,
And, ere the evening's close,
Much had been wrought

That absence, time, nor sorrow could efface;
And on the brow of each
A seal was set, to teach
That if we chase

A phantom danger, real may be near.
They never thought of this.
The rosebud, and the kiss,
So long, so dear,

That followed it—the simple pledge of love—
Awoke the wish that slept
In the heart's secret crypt;
Nor God above,

Nor man below, could check the burning flood
Of passion sweeping on,
Until all sense was gone!
O treacherous bud!

If all thy leaves were multiplied as is
The sand on the sea-shore,
Our tears for thee were more
Than all of this!

'Twas offer'd—taken—and the thoughts flew back
To that it emblems oft;
And all the emotions soft
That in the track

Of passion follow, crowded round them there,
In the still eve; their eyes
Grew full, and the warm sighs
That seem to bear

The very soul of love on their light wings,
Flew from her parted lips;
Can time—can death eclipse
The light that brings

The memory of that moment back to each,
With all its life of life,
Its passion and its strife?
How cold is speech!

How feebly, dimly can our words express
What we have strongly felt!
Not mine the tongue to melt
To tenderness

The listener's heart, and draw the genial flood
Of pity from cold fountains, else
These lines would stir full many a pulse :—
O treacherous bud!

So simple wert thou, that no tremor crossed
Them thou didst lead all silently
Down to that ever-surging sea
Where all was lost!

A WINTER LYRIC.

I.

Comrades, 'tis a stormy winter,
And the snow-drift rises higher—
Quick, and fling a larger splinter
On the fire!
Let the loud wind moaning o'er us—
O'er the warm and shingled thatch—
Hear our Bacchanalian chorus,
Glee and catch!

II.

Comrades, list the wintry battle—
See the white and hideous gloom!
How the doors and windows rattle
In the room!
Draw the curtains—dice and drinking,
Woman's lip, and wit refined—
These will save the sin of thinking
Heaven unkind!

III.

Comrades, 'till the dreary morning
  Shine above the waste of snow,
Let delight, at prudence scorning,
    Rule below!
Fill the flagon—each a brimmer,
  Ruby red and fiery strong!
Blood is cold, but it will simmer
    Before long!

IV.

Comrades, fill a deeper flagon!
  See the golden apples gleam!
Fruit of joy!—O, slay the dragon
    Guarding them!
Life 's an auction; please the palate,
  Purchase every costly toy;
And 'till death lets fall his mallet,
    Bid for joy!

V.

Comrades, hear the hollow moaning
  Of the tempest o'er the wold!

Earth is white with fright and groaning
In the cold.
Some there be, perchance, who wander
Shivering, houseless, loveless, lone;
These are thoughts to make us fonder
Of our own!

VI.

Clinking glasses! what surpasses
The rich melody ye chime!
How ye brighten, cheer and lighten
Winter time!
Woman's lip is ripe and melting
Dearer far than summer's rose,
For, when storms around are pelting,
See! it glows!

VII.

Woman fairest! Laura dearest!
Love you not the whirling storm?
Let it mutter, while we utter
Whispers warm!
Nestle closer! Let thy tresses
Bathe and shade my panting heart.

Winter, bringing such caresses,
Ne'er depart!

VIII.

Friends, brim up a richer beaker
Than ye e'er have quaffed before,
For the storm strikes, bleak and bleaker,
On the door!
'Till the lightning cleave the shingle,
And the snow-drift chill the bowl,
Sing, and drink, and kiss, and mingle
Soul with soul!

THE MYSTIC VOICE.

I.

Earth is a realm of ceaseless change
Where forms are merged in fresher forms,
And still the beautiful and strange
Are cradled in destructive storms;

For Nature's alchemies impart
  New life to all transmuted things,
And lend the flesh-decaying heart
  The eternal spirit's tireless wings.

II.

The sordid shrine, whose vestal fire
  Burns dim within the grosser frame,
May perish, but the rays aspire,
  And reach once more from whence they came;
We pass, as through the entrancéd flood,
  From Egypt's toil to Canaan's bloom,
And with the sacrifice of blood
  We find new life beyond the tomb.

III.

Still, through the vast and deepening void,
  Like sentient flames the Spirits come,
Eternal, changeless, undestroyed,
  And speaking, though the grave be dumb.
Within the soul their vital spell
  Reveals the fount from whence it rose,
The beautiful—the terrible—
  The strange preamble to the close!

IV.

And thou, whose soul with ardor filled,
  Hast seen the fire, and heard the voice,
For whom the future field is tilled
  And waits the harvest, make thy choice!
It lies before thee; struggle—strive;
  Thou canst not beat conviction back;
Weak fugitive from higher life,
  Eternal wings pursue thy track!

V.

Ah, traitor soul! for whom in vain
  The veil of Heaven was drawn aside,
As if to give the impassioned brain
  An ampler scope, a steadier guide!
Thou slave of sense, still madly hurled
  Across the unfruitful waste of years!
Thou stagnant ship, whose white sails furled
  Rot idly, dropping stagnant tears!

VI.

Awake! Beyond the impassive grave,
  The spheres of being spread afar,

Circle on circle, wave on wave,
An ocean, where each freighted star
Is as a bark that bears along,
From suffering to the blissful shore,
The beautiful, the good, the strong,
Their term of sad probation o'er.

VII.

Earth dies; and Heaven with purer light
Prepares to clothe our mystic orb.
The Spirits move in viewless flight
To cheer the dying, and absorb
The falsehoods which have mingled ill
And pain in life's enchanted bowl.
Heaven's only keys are human Will
A striving Love, an earnest Soul!

THE MIDNIGHT WATCH.

'Tis late—but thus I muse and read
While all around in slumber nod;
O Night! to those who will but heed,
Thou art the sermon-time of God!

The house is hushed—the smouldering fire
  Burns low within the glowing grate,
And one by one the lamps expire—
  Now let me meditate !

The house is hushed—a fearful calm
  That bids the spirit look within—
And solitude is bane or balm,
  Proportioned to our weight of sin ;
The day, its deeds, our future hopes,
  Are meeted all with equal weight ;
And Conscience her true mirror opes
  When the night is wearing late.

How hushed ! The moaning breeze evokes
  A thrill of terror—ghostly—dim !
The grim clock deals some fearful strokes
  On Time's outspeeding cherubim ;
The muffled Hours with hurrying feet
  Still bear to the eternal gate
Reproachful thoughts, an offering meet
  From those who meditate.

No sound, save when the wainscot mouse,
  Or crumbling cinder bids us start—

Sepulchral silence in the house,
  And turmoil in the sleepless heart.
O dreams of youth! ye seem to creep,
  In bodiless vapors from the grate,
Round one to whom the eternal sleep
  Comes welcome, if not late.

TO LAURA.

We must not show the hidden bower
  Where love's high feasts are holden;
We must not let another see
  The secret flower, perfumed and golden,
That twinkles on the shadowed lea
  For you and me,
        Dear Laura!

We must not show the priceless gem,
  That gleams in pleasure's casket;
No jealous eye its light may see,

Lest those who envy us should ask it,
Or question how it came to be
With you and me,
Dear Laura!

We must not show the hidden spring
Where passion cools its fever;
We must not let the slightest sound
Betray our joy, but be for ever
Mute as the woods that wave around
Our hallowed ground,
My Laura!

O could we flee, like doves, afar
From custom's iron bondage,
To some rich isle in the southern sea,
There, in the wood's enwoven frondage,
With souls and passions linked, to be
Unwatched, and free!
Dear Laura!

Still, in the world be cold, reserved,
With social fetters laden!
The humble minstrel, what is he,

To win the heart of this rich maiden ?
But there are hours—thank heaven there be !—
For you and me,
My Laura !

I would not change my pride of song
For all a prince's treasure ;
Not all the wealth beneath the sea
Could yield its lord such passionate pleasure,
As when, upon the shadowed lea,
I pluck the golden flower with thee,
And kiss the gem which none may see,
But you and me,
My Laura !

THE MOURNERS.

But yesternight, his arms were braced
With fixed resolve, and courage high ;
The sword and buckler, seized in haste,
With vows to conquer or to die.

See! where his country's pennons fly
Above the Autumn's trampled waste,
The chosen Chief of Liberty
In Freedom's chosen vanguard placed!

The smoke of battle clears away!
The host he led, with victory crowned,
Return the conquerors of the day,
And all is mirth and gladness round!
But whence that wild and wailing sound,
Amid the shout and revel gay?
A voice as if from the profound
Shrill-piercing on its heavenward way!

" He comes not! He will come no more!
" Say! lives he, though with wounds oppressed?
" This dreadful day of conflict o'er,
" Why miss I now his pluméd crest?
" O that I shared his tranquil rest;
" Nor felt the fiery waves that pour
" The tide of memory through my breast,
" Against the heart's forsaken shore!

" He comes not! But a month has passed,—
" One summer moon, since we were wed!

"One wingéd month that fled so fast!
"It can not be, that he is dead.
"These racking tortures in my head—
"This heart, as if with ice o'ercast—
"I dream!—O God!—He is not dead—
"He comes!—My love returns at last!"

O balm of Madness! kindly given
To griefs that scorn the patient tear—
O ye wild dreams that wing from Heaven
Betwixt our souls and all we fear,
Now, hover gently!—hover here,
Ere life from its last pulse be driven!
Nor let the fatal truth appear,
That all she loved from earth is riven!

With trembling step she seeks the ground
Where horse and man together lie—
The field of death, with scarce a sound
Except the vulture's sated cry,
Or the last deep expiring sigh
Of shattered manhood; and around
She casts a calm, untroubled eye
O'er many a corse-encumbered mound!

A milk-white steed is standing there
  With nostril wide and quivering limb!
O Madness! shield her from despair!
  That panting steed belonged to him.
  Her lips grow white, her eyes grow dim,
The film of Death they seem to bear—
  And yet, as through a garden trim,
She picks her steps with dainty care!

She stoops with slow, unconscious grace,
  And gazes vacantly awhile
Upon the cold, unanswering face
  That ne'er met hers without a smile.
  So sweetly Madness can beguile
The burning heart of all its pain!
  So Fancy build her greenest isle
In Death and Sorrow's tideless main!

I see her pale lips shrink and quiver,
  As they to his cold brow are pressed;
She calls him!—and a dreary shiver
  Convulses now her marble breast!
  That harrowing shriek of deep unrest
Bears forth her life on its wide river.
  Beneath yon old rude cross they rest,
In Death's long slumber knit for ever!

THE STARS OF MEMORY.

In retrospection's dream I see
  The waste of years that stretch afar
Into the dim eternity,
  With here and there a shining star;
Sweet stars of memory beaming o'er
  The sepulchres of perished Hope;
And backward turn I more and more,
  As gloomier paths before me ope.

I turn me back and watch the sky
  Grow ruddy in the youthful dawn;
I watch the glorious shadows fly
  Across the lake and o'er the lawn;
The evening clouds are turned to gray,
  Though streaked by many a crimson bar,
And darkness comes, yet fleets away,
  And leaves behind one glittering star!

It leaves,—but not the star of morn,
  Whose pale beams merge in fuller light,
When flowers and birds seem newly born,
  And freshened by the dews of night;

That loveliest star for ever set,
  No second morrow bids arise;
And sadly, vainly, we regret
  The lustre that has left our skies!

The Past was as an easy road
  That led us down a hill of flowers,
Where every opening vista showed
  But brighter streams and greener bowers;
We reach at length the barren plain
  Where man contests the race of life,
We join the struggle, feel the pain,
  Yet love the excitement of the strife!

We love the strife that makes the tide
  Of passion swell within the heart;
Nor deem we, in our youthful pride,
  Ambition's pulse can e'er depart.
We love it, while our hearts are strung
  With high romance and ancient lore;
We love it, while our hopes are young,
  And paint a brighter scene before.

But, as we wander on and on,
  And weary of the loveless life,

We turn to find the flowers are gone
  Beneath the mailéd hoofs of strife;
We wake to know that manhood brings
  The pain that finds no balm in tears;
We wake to know that conscience stings;
  We wake to mourn the bygone years!

The stubborn soul is loath to quit
  The dream that it hath made its god,
And—forced to own its misery—yet
  Pursues the path it once hath trod,
Looks round it with a careless eye
  On others equally unblest,
And pinions every struggling sigh
  Within the portals of the breast.

We wander on—the early hope
  In which, beyond the sultry plain,
We saw serener vistas ope,
  Experience proves is false and vain;
For ever with a lengthening chain,
  For ever with a darker pall,
We journey to the grave in pain,
  And see our fellow-bondsmen fall.

Pride checks the tear, and with a frown
  Would chase the phantom Grief away;
The snows of age come thickening down,
  And chill and bleaker grows the way;
We speak what we would fain unsay,
  But pride steps in with ready art,
And in a semblance of the gay
  We veil the anguish of the heart.

Amid the gloom we gladly turn,
  When none may mock our silent tears,
To where the stars of memory burn
  Above the joys of other years;
And Fancy in the dusk uprears
  The radiant forms of perished worth,
Which we have borne on flowery biers,
  And laid within the lap of earth.

O stars of memory! ever shine,
  And brighter as our joys decay!
Still shed your influence divine
  To guide us on our lonely way!
Bright stars of memory! shine for ever,
  Like beacons o'er the troubled main,
Until in Lethe's tranquil river
  We anchor from the storms of pain!

A COLLEGE SONG.

Well, the world goes round for ever,
  Whether we are sad, or gay;
Floats the cloud and rolls the river;
  Should we pine our lives away?
  Night usurps the throne of day,
And, when morning's lances quiver,
  O'er the mountains flies away,
But returns at sunset ever!
  Earth alternates night and day,
          Grave and gay!

If the world so little care us,
  Why should we regard the world?
Still its flowery meadows bear us,
  And the star-tent is unfurled.
  Even the stars from heaven are hurled;
And the grasp of death will tear us
  From the tree round which we curled,—
From the tree of life will tear us,
  Round which our affections curled,—
          From the world!

Comrades! while the earth so alters,
  Wintry frost and blossom spring,

Foolish he who doubts and falters ;
  Pleasure flies on rapid wing,—
  Seize it ere you feel the sting!
Bow your heart to passions' altars,
  Let your soul its incense fling,
Ere the gilded pagod falters,
  Ere you feel the hidden sting,
          Of the wing!

Comrades! soon the world will leave us
  Stranded on the shores of time ;
Years of all our joys bereave us ;
  Age is like the serpent-slime,
  Staining roses in their prime.
Every day will deeper grieve us,
  Every parting hour will chime
A knell for the sweet hopes that leave us
  Buried in the by-gone time,—
          Hear it chime!

Comrades! seize the passing moment
  Lent us by Eternity!
Use it wisely—for 'tis so lent,
  As a drop from out the sea,
  Rolling backward instantly!

Age advances. gray and low bent,
  As the waves of pleasure flee,—
Drives us to our latest moment,
  To the dread eternity—
  To that vast and trackless sea,
Over which the clouds are low bent,
  And uncounted shadows flee.

THE RUBY.

[In acknowledgment of a ring received from J. T. Trowbridge—better known to literature and fame as "Paul Creyton."]

I.

Dear Creyton! when the listless pen
  Sways idly in my wearied fingers,
And round my throbbing heart and brain
  No ray of brighter fancy lingers,
I catch the sparkle of the stone
  That speaks of friendship undecaying,
And straight the clouds aside are thrown;
  A fresher light is round me playing.

II.

They say, that talismans of old
   Protected from all hidden dangers;
That spirits lay within the gold,
   At once protectors and avengers.
The ring you gave, like these, may prove
   The bane of grief, the source of pleasure;
For all is pleasing that can move
   Remembrance of an absent treasure!

III.

Like friendship's fire, the brilliant toy,
   Deep set in memory's golden circle,
Throws back the ruddy beam of joy,
   And in the dullest night will sparkle.
The ring, like memory—endless both—
   Its warmth from out my heart is getting,
And, like myself, of foreign growth,
   Rejoices in a Yankee setting.

IV.

My muse—a woman, and you know
   The female heart inclines to jewels—

Whene'er she wants "full speed" to go,
  Her engine at the ruby fuels :
The pistons of alternate rhyme
  Move up and down with steady motion—
The train of thought, defying time,
  Speeds on through earth and air and ocean !

V.

The Koh-i-noor in Britain's crown
  Is India's blood-mark set upon her ;
The sapphire clasp of beauty's gown
  Perchance was purchased by dishonor ;
The miser's gold is dim with tears,
  And rusted thick with cent. per-centage :
My ring then, clearly, it appears
  O'er these can claim immense advantage !

VI.

The mine wherein the ruby lay,
  Was filled with geologic spirits :
The gnome, you know—as poets say—
  The treasury of earth inherits.
So friendship lies within the heart,
  Possessed by wild, ideal fancies,

'Till favoring fortune tear apart
 The veil with genial necromancies.

VII.

The lips—by Cyprian Venus planned—
 Convey love's telegraphic greeting;
But friendship meets us hand to hand
 To feel how either's pulse is beating.
And on that hand the ring I hold,
 As prized as talisman by dervise;
And may that hand be foul and cold,
 When 't is not warmly at thy service!

THE CHALLENGE CUP.

"Fill high the bowl with Samian wine!"
 So runs the high old Grecian hymn;
Give me a pail of ocean brine,
 And fill the beaker to the brim!

Let all the Nereids, fair and slim,
  From out their pearly grots advance,
While bright mermaidens lead the dim
  And flickering whirl of Neptune's dance.

On such an eve was Venus born,
  Where Cypria's shore the blue tide laves,
And now the Peris' hands adorn
  With amber buds our heroes' graves;
Call the Typhoon from those grim caves,
  Where still he winds his wondrous horn,
Let mirth above the moonlight waves
  Lead from her couch the roseate morn.

To-night the ocean cup is won,
  The sway from Albion's shore hath passed,
The race of Albion's glory's done—
  Wind, Typhoon, wind thy loudest blast!
Come from your coral couches fast,
  Ye slumbering tenants of the main,
Your starry shrouds around you cast—
  Come forth, and join the festal train!

Glory to God! The stars arise
  In bright effulgence o'er the deep.

The vaulted heaven is full of eyes,
 And tranced and mute the billows sleep!
Wrapped in their clouds, our martyrs sweep
 In shadowy radiance through the skies,
And the wild-bounding dolphin leap
 Like silvery shafts around the prize!

'Tis done! 'tis won!—the cup is ours!
 No blood hath stained its virgin rim,
No widow's curse around it lowers,
 No orphan's tears have made it dim!
Higher and higher let the hymn
 Ascend from our wild western bowers,
While unto Liberty and God
 We dedicate our future powers!

WEBSTER.

Gone! and the world may never hear again
 The grand old music of thy wondrous speech,
 Striking far deeper than the mind can reach
Into the hearts and purposes of men!

Gone! and the helm that in thy Roman hand
Drove the stout vessel through the blinding storm,
Scarce to a feebler guidance will conform,
When waves beat high, and ropes break strand by strand.

Gone! we are like old men whose infant eyes
Familiar grew with some vast pyramid;
Even as we gaze, earth yawns, and it is hid.
A long, wide desert mocks the empty skies!

MORE LIGHT.

More light—more light—more light!
This is the cry of unhappy humanity,
This is the prayer of poor blinded humanity,
Groping in passion, in pain and inanity
Round the bleak walls of the prison of vanity;
Everywhere seeking a ray of Divinity,
Everywhere finding the terrible Trinity:

Darkness, and Dolor, and Doubt inexpressible—
Numbness, and Dumbness, and Pain inexpressible—
All that is terrorful, all that is horrorful,
Doubts irrepressible, woe unendurable,
Tears that fall laughingly, smiles that are sorrowful!
Longing and gleams of superior existences,
Voices that whisper from infinite distances,
(Mystical distances! soul-haunted distances!)
Beauty that flings back the folds of a cerement,
Skeletons veiled in the garments of merriment,
All that is exquisite, all that is wonderful,
Earth a vast Theatre, over and under full,
Full to the brim of discordant existences,
Matter and Spirit, and Powers and Resistances.
Everywhere opposites: Anguish and Levity,
Mortal Reality, hoped Immortality,
Art for long years, and man's life but a brevity!
O, in this shadowed and whispering night,
This mystical stage with its curtain of night,
Grant us Thy wisdom—Thy comfort—Thy light—
Grant us more light—more light!

ITALIAN FREEDOM.

"Insurrection! let the grand word pass from city to city, from town to town, from village to village, like the electric current. Arouse! arise! awake to the crusade fever, all ye who have Italian hearts — Italian arms!"—*Mazzini.*

The hands that move on Freedom's clock
  Already strike the appointed hour;
The tocsin sounds, the people flock,
  Majestic in their banded power.
Italia wakes! From town to town
  The leaders cry, "To arms! obey us!"
The Austrian sword, the Papal crown
  Reel on the verge of chaos.

Up, all who bear the Latin heart!
  Up, all who love the vengeful joy!
Let your fierce wrath, like lightning, dart
  Upon the tyrants and destroy!
Up! from the Tiber to the Arve,
  Let Insurrection's tocsin toll,
While weaponed arms united carve
  A path for the free soul!

Let Austria's cut-throat legions learn
  To feel and fear the Roman rage!

Let the fierce Pontiff's eyes discern
  The dawn of the millennial age!
Tell fratricidal France her hordes
  No more shall bid Italia weep.
Reap a full harvest with your swords,
  And garner what you reap!

Up, Latins! by the foulest wrongs
  That ever suffering manhood bore!
By ruffian steel and priestly thongs
  Imbued in patriot gore!
By every scaffold through the land!
  By dungeon vault and leprous spy!
Up! up! and with an armèd hand
  Strike down this living lie!

No more be scourged by priestly cords,
  No more be ruled by foreign steel,
No more be robbed by foreign lords,—
  Arise!—the tyrants reel.
Expect no mercy, breath no sigh
  In this last desperate throe for life;
Let "Death or Victory" be the cry,
  And war unto the knife!

A RUSHING MELODY.

THE FEAST OF TURKEY AND A FLOW OF RHYME.

I.

So far as I can reason down
  The complex Eastern question,
A Turkey, done exceeding brown,
  Would suit the Czar's digestion.
Be trussed it must with bayonets first,
  And peppered well with powder;
Then, sliced out into provinces,
  'Twill make a famous chowder.

II.

Poor Turkey cannot bear a yoke,
  Though turkey-eggs bear pullets;
Nor can the Sultan see the joke,
  Of making his eggs bullets,

Though he has got a hundred wives,
  He dearly loves Moll Davia;
And Galatz is the kind of gal
  He wouldn't part to save you.

III.

Though men shake off the Russian wiles,
  Still, Men-shi-koff is great, Sir!
And Dardan ells are crooked miles,
  Although they call them "strait," Sir.
The Sultan in his harem sits,
  While things go harum-scarum.
He gets in-Sultin' messages,
  And cannot choose but bear 'em.

IV.

The Turk appeals to God and Truth,
  But suffers ne'ertheless he;
For Gortschakoff, beside the Pruth,
  At Jassy, gives him Jessy.
With Gortscha-koff and Menschi-koff,
  His breast has got a stuffing,
And if he cannot shake them off—
  These coughs will nail his coffin.

V.

The Czar is clad in costly furs,
From Vashka and Yakaka;
While Turkey's sole defence from "koffs"
Is Redschid Ali Pacha.
The Sultan to the Prophet prays—
No profit comes a-near him;
And though his Porte be called Sublime,
It has not strength to cheer him.

VI.

He prays to Mecca, but he finds
The mecha-nism is rusty;
His prayer cannot unlock the gate,
And so the Portë grows crusty:
His Viziers put their visors down,
And will not face the tussle;
Alas! the faithful Mussulmans
Have neither brain nor muscle.

VII.

Dis-turbin' hands his turban touch—
His hookah it is hooked, Sir;
And soon, before a Cossack fire,
Will Turkey's goose be cooked, Sir.

His Mamelukes to mammy look,
  Nor are for battle pressing;
His Pashas of a dozen tails
  Have tales the most distressing.

VIII.

His Dragomans can't drag a man
  To fight—the Turks ain't stupid,—
His Eunuchs are as impotent,
  For Mars as eke for Cupid.
There's not a man in his Divan,
  In honor's van will die, Sir;
Before the storm that Bruin brews,
  The turkey soon must fly, Sir.

IX.

Though England promised men and mon-
  Ey, now she goes for snacks, Sir,
Preferring Turkey underdone,
  To fighting with Cossacks, Sir!
Old Nick may send his serfs to fight
  From Kostroma and Kausardz,
While Louis in the *Parc aux Cerfs*,
  Is shooting turkey-buzzards.

X.

The Cossacks are a savage horde,
But Turks with them can cope ill;
St. Petersburg obeys the sword,
Not so Constantinople.
The Turks are called to daily prayer
From minaret and steeple,
So well-informed they are, they're called
The constant "*I* know" people.

XI.

The Sea of Marmora is small,
A sea-ton in the neck, Sir,
Which joins the European head
Unto the Asian wreck, Sir;
The Turk, I fear, must cross it soon,
To mar more utter ruin,
And this is all I know about
The tempest that is Bruin.

XII.

The Turks gave shelter to Kossuth—
For this esteemed their souls are;

May they ne'er know a Hungary day
  Partitioned as the Poles are!
May Allah and the Christian's God
  Confound unchristian Czars, Sir,
And may the Crescent moon be girt
  With bright Columbian stars, Sir!

THE RHYMER'S RITUAL.

Of all the kinds of snobbish rhyme
  That fail to please or tickle us,
  The worst and most ridiculous
  Is when young bards be-trickle us
With "tears" they shed "in early time."

The poet's task, when understood,
  Is not with pain to fetter us,
  And dolefully be-letter us;
  It is to touch and better us
With glintings of a gentler mood.

What cares a steam-electric age
For narratives Byronical ?
It rather loves to chronicle
A witty thing laconical,
Flung lightly down upon the page.

We all have griefs enough to spare
Without a man inditing 'em
And metrically writing 'em—
The wiser plan is slighting 'em,
A hearty laugh can conquer care.

A grain of Burns is worth a mint
Of Byron's dolorosity.
Tom Hood's immense jocosity
Beats Milton's ponderosity.
True wit has always wisdom in 't.

Long since, an inexperienced fool,
I loved the hyperbolical—
The Sue-Dumas-Sand-Gaulical
Creations melancholical—
The writings of the "thrilling school."

'Tis strange that while of real grief
We all have such immensities,
Men still should have propensities
For reading wild intensities
Of agonies beyond belief.

For me, I will not read the stuff
  Of German tales—too deep a bit,—
  That will not let me sleep a bit.
  If e'er I want to weep a bit
My life is tragical enough.

Let every male and female bard
  Write merrily if possible,
  Or make pretensions plausible
  To that which may be causable
Of smiling readers—'tis not hard.

The lightest pleasaunce of the mind
  Outweighs its deepest polity;
  Whate'er awakens jollity
  Can ne'er be deemed frivolity
By those who are not wilful-blind.

I'd rather think the lines I penned
  Made one hour pass more cheerily,
  More lightly and less wearily,
  Than know that readers drearily
Went blubbering on from end to end.

A BROADWAY BELLE.

I saw her in the window,
  She was fairest of the fair;
I thought it were no sin to
  Kneel down before her there.
Her dress was brightest, fullest,
  That e'er by zone was bound;
And her fan—it was the coolest
  That e'er shed fragrance round.

She turned around—but slowly,
  With a cold, unfeeling grace,
Although a hundred lowly
  Adored her radiant face.
Her hair might claim the far a-
  Doration of the world,
With its gold and pearl tiara
  Above her ringlets curled.

There were brilliant toys around her
  Of velvet and of silk,
As fair as those which bound her
  White shoulders—white as milk,

Her eyes were bright, but rayless,
They lacked the vital spark,—
And lovely—could I say less?
The mind—the soul was dark!

" O loveliest of the gentle
And fair!"—I did repeat—
" Behold me! I have bent all
My passions to thy feet!
Grant,—and the boon entrances
Your poet—lover—slave,
One of your kindly glances
To cheer me toward my grave!"

Thus wrapt in love and wonder
I stood before the shrine,
When a voice like summer thunder
Disturbed this trance of mine:
It cried—" Are you astonished
That the girl expression lacks?
Henceforward be admonished—
Your idol is of wax!"

A VERY TENDER BALLAD,

AND ALL TOO TRUE.

Of Sarah Brown and Geordie Mairs,
The love I will relate;
The saddest history is theirs,
That has been writ of late.

Of Geordie Mairs and Sarah Brown
I sing the mournful fate;
Ye lovers, list, in field and town,
And profit ere too late!

PART FIRST.

In Morristown lived Sarah Brown,
A maid of scant sixteen;
And Geordie Mairs his witching airs
Her youthful heart did win.

But Mr. Brown did grimly frown—
Old fathers are such bears—
Upon the love of Sarah Brown
For sprightly Master Mairs,

And then the couple did revolve,
  A scheme to cheat the sire,
For it was Geordie's firm resolve
  To win her, or expire.

From Morristown with Sarah Brown,
  Young Geordie did elope,
And for to pass to Worcester, Mass.,
  And wed it was his hope.

They came away at break of day,
  Did George and Sally Brown;
They blessed their stars and took the cars
  For Gotham's mighty town.

And in the city's sordid throng,
  Its pomp, and pride, and pain,
They moved, like an unwritten song
  Within the poet's brain.

Through groaning street and glittering mart
  They moved as in a dream—
Twin-Siamesians of the heart,
  Two stars with blended beam.

The waves of life that surged on high,
  But rocked the skiff of love ;
It flew betwixt the sea and sky
  With the white wings of a dove.

It bore them on by Passion isles,
  Exempt from human ills ;
It drifted down through green defiles
  Of myrtle-covered hills.

It slept on memory's waveless mere,
  And, looking down, they saw
Two smiling faces drawing near,
  As theirs did nearer draw.

Oh ! woe is me for Geordie Mairs !
  For Sally Brown I weep !
They do engross my muse's cares,
  And bar mine eyes of sleep.

Oh ! woe is me for Sally Brown,
  And Geordie Mairs her mate !—
Why linger they in Gotham town,
  While " the Goth is at the gate ?"

PART SECOND.

O, fierce the frown of Mr. Brown,
As breakfast hour drew near,
And yet no Sally brought his gown,
Nor plumped his easy chair.

A rougher wrinkle scarred his brow
As breakfast hour drew near,
And yet no slippers waited now,
Nor daughter did appear.

" Ho! Sally, come!—what ails the girl,
Or is she sick or dead ?
By holy heaven! 'tis nearly seven,
And not yet breakfasted!

" What, Sarah! Ho! Run up, and call
The sluttish vixen down!"—
So said, unto her brother Paul,
The senior Mister Brown.

Full lightly Paul did mount the stairs,
And searched in every cranny;
" I'll bet she's gone with Geordie Mairs—
As good a match as any!

" Last ' Fourth'—let's see—he gave a V,
   And New-Year's Day a Ten;
' Thanksgiving,' too, I got a Three,
   And on my birthday One."

So pondered Paul, remembering all
   The heaps of cash and cake
Which Geordie Mairs had given to him,
   For his sweet sister's sake.

" She's gone, I swow! I've hunted through
   The rooms from last to first,
And here's a note addressed to you,
   'Twill tell the best or worst!"

The hand that swayed the pen was light,
   The ink was radiant blue.
'Twas traced upon a sheet of white,
   As if her soul looked through—

As if her radiant eyes outshook,
   Upon her pallid cheek,
The rays of that inquiring look
   She did not dare to speak.

"O father, dear! how much I fear
  To draw your curses down!
'Tis pain to live, till you forgive,
  And bless your Sally——Brown."

"O father, dear! but see! a tear
  My maiden name doth blot,
So let me be forgiven of thee,
  And be my fault forgot.

"I cannot love but Geordie Mairs;
  Yet you would have me wed
Old Asa Parr! 'Twere better far,
  Your Sally Brown were dead!

"O sweeter far if daisy turf,
  Grew o'er your Sally's sleep,
Or, down below the dirging surf,
  She slumbered in the deep!

"Sweeter that worms upon me fed,
  While the black earth pressed above,
Than live to share a hated bed,
  And loathe a husband's love.

" O father! turn to the grassy mound,
Where my sainted mother lies,
With meadow-sweet at her silent feet,
And violets o'er her eyes;

" O, kindly look on her blossomed grave,
My hands have trimmed it fresh,
And let her guardian spirit save
The daughter of her flesh!

" Forgive me! would you not repine,
To see me waste away,
Still paling in the heart's decline,
And wasting day by day?

" You would, you would! and tho' I know
'Tis wrong to thwart your will,
The highest duties here below
Have higher duties still.

" E'en though a father order me,
I may not swear above,
To love the man I most abhor,
And hate the man I love.

"So now I go with Geordie Mairs,
To be his faithful wife,
To worship him and cling to him,
As she to you in life.

"O, could you know what bosom ties,
The suit you urged has riven,
You would relent, and exercise
The quality of heaven.

"Forgiveness for an erring child;
Ah me! I dread your frown;
Your smile can bless with happiness,
Your George and Sarah Brown!"

PART THIRD.

A wrathy man the father grew,
And fiercely did he ramp;
"By heaven! the hussy yet shall rue,
That she vamosed the camp.

"I will not eat, I will not tire,
Until I bring her back;
I'll put the telegraphic wire,
And sheriff on her track!

"I'll kill her if she be his wife,
  I'll kill her husband too—
I'll take a cowhide for the priest
  And clerk, and put them through.

"My hat and cane! By death and birth!
  The jade shall learn her duty;
I'll teach her there are things on earth
  More dear than dreams of beauty.

"What! run away, at break of day,
  From such a loving father!
Elope, and ask me to forgive!
  'Tis cool—refreshing—rather."

He seized his hat and crushed it flat
  Upon his wrinkled brow;
He seized his cane which bent amain
  Beneath his pressure now.

He seized his coat and struggled hard,
  Until he squeezed it on,
Then down the steps and through the yard
  Old Mister Brown has gone.

* * * * * * *

O ye, who now in Gotham seem
  To taste the promised bliss,
Why did no bird or fairy dream
  Acquaint your souls of this ?

O, why no hovering angel's lip
  Forebode the coming doom ?
O, why should Love so harshly nip
  His first-begotten bloom ?

O Geordie Mairs, descend the stairs,
  And quickly leave the town ;
Right quickly pass to Worcester, Mass.,
  Or lose your Sally Brown.

* * * * * * *

Swift as the bolt the Thunderer flings,
  The father on them sweeps ;
Revenge still flies on lightning wings,
  While Love, soft dallying, creeps.

Yea ! Mr. Brown arrived in town,
  To mar the lovers' peace ;
He published an advertisement,
  And started the police.

And he described them inch by inch,
  The dress that either wears,
The cherry gown of Sally Brown,
  The vest of Geordie Mairs.

A crimson vest bechained with gold,
  A Kossuth hat and feather,
An olive coat, surprising pants,
  And a crimson tie together.

PART FOURTH.

'Tis four P. M., on Courtlandt pier,
  And porters bellow loud,
While newsboys rush distractedly
  Through the distracted crowd.

The Worcester line is bound to start
  At four, from Gotham town,
And thither with a beating heart
  Go George and Sally Brown.

" I wish to pass to Worcester, Mass.,"
  Said George, and gave a Five;
The clerk replied, " Your change—'tis late
  You'd better look alive.

How could he be alive, I say,
  When nearly dead with fright?
For as he stepped upon the plank,
  Brown, senior, met his sight.

As Homer wrapped the wrangling gods
  In clouds of sable hue,
Defying even a Yankee stare
  To pierce the curtain through;

So on the luckless loving pair,
  The father and the crowd,
I turn a rhyming cuttle-fish,
  And raise an inky cloud.

But through the cloud and from the crowd,
  We heard a voice of moan;
The father's curses, long and loud,
  And Geordie's pleading tone.

A silver voice is pleading, too,
  Alas! to deafest ears;
The "stars" of the policemen heed
  No "music of the spheres."

And ladies who are passengers
  Are taking Sally's part;
But all in vain—no power can gain
  The father's flinty heart.

O Love! for ever claiming souls
  To worship at your shrine;
Among your host of martyrs write
  This loving pair of mine!

Among your noblest martyr band,
  Who bore misfortune's frown,
Inscribe in memory's roundest hand,
  "G. Mairs," and "Sarah Brown."

"THE NYMPH OF LURLEIBERGH."

I.

In Lurleibergh's deep-shadowed vale,
  Where all the Rhine's blue waters meet,
A maiden sat, as fair and pale
  As were the lilies at her feet,

Her hair in wild profusion flowing
  From roses vainly wreathed above,
To hide the gentle bosom, glowing
  With mingled thoughts of fear and love!
O Nymph of Lurleiburgh! thy lute,
Why stands it thus untouched and mute?
What pensive shadows cloud thine eye,
And cheat the moments as they fly?
Thou art too young, too fair for pain
To dim the smile and thrill the brain,
Too pure thou seem'st for thought of ill,
Yet sad thou art and pensive still!

II.

Yea, thou art sad; although no tear
  Bedews thy silken-fringéd lid,
And all the more will sorrow sear
  When thus in mute endurance hid:
Thine eyes are fixed upon the river,
  As past thy feet its waters roll,
And, wild as are its billows, quiver
  The tides of passion in thy soul!
O Nymph of Lurleibergh! the crown
Of flowers you wear will wither soon!
The lute's harmonious chord will slack,

And youth—once flown—comes never back;
The gushing waters pure and sweet,
That pour their tribute to thy feet,
Soon pass the bowers of trellised vine,
And perish in the stormy brine!

III.

We should not waste in tears the hours
  Of youth, that all too fleetly flow;
In spring, the fields are decked with flowers
  And wintry age is capped with snow;
And thou art in the spring of being,
  And thou should'st be as light and gay
As is the lark when upward fleeing
  To bathe his pinions in the ray
That calls the bluebell from the meadow,
And steeps the hill in sultry shadow,—
That bathes the morning lake in fire,
And tips with gold the village spire.
I too have felt the hopeless void
Of pleasures lost when most enjoyed,
And learned, alas! that tears are vain
To wash such memories from the brain.

A WINDY DISSERTATION.

Two breezes in the forest met,
  A little way from town;
The one was blowing up to it,
  The other blowing down:
They whispered kindly through the trees,
  Through foliage, branch, and fork,
And that one was a country breeze,
  And this was from New-York.

They tossed the crimson leaves about,
  And whirling danced around;
They laughed to see the forest rout
  Fall eddying to the ground;
To shaking nests and stripping boughs
  And such like sports they fell,
Till, tired at last, one said, "Suppose
  What each has seen we tell!"

The country breeze—the sweeter far—
  Full pleasantly replied,
"I've driven upon my cloudy car
  O'er landscapes fair and wide.

I've seen the harvest gathered home
   By ruddy men and maids;
I've cooled me in the cataract's foam
   And slept in quiet glades.

"But most of all I loved to force
   My way through those old woods,
Upon whose murmurs, warm and hoarse,
   No human voice intrudes;
'Tis pleasant, too, to breast the top
   Of yonder snow-clad hills,
Then down into the valleys drop
   And chase the flying rills.

"O'er lakes that slumbered in the sun
   Like mirrors broad and bright,
My path has been a pleasant one
   Of perfume and of light.
And now I seek the city—there,
   I hear, are glorious things—
Come, tell to me, my sister fair,
   Where you have spread your wings?"

So loudly then the other sighed
   She made the branches sway;

The squirrel, perching overhead,
  Affrighted leaped away.
"O sister! blest hath been your lot;
  Far different mine hath been!
Now hear my tale, and you will not
  Desert the forest green.

"Condemned by fate, I wandered round
  Yon pile of smoky brick;
And men and mud were all I found,
  And both have made me sick:
The towering chimneys volumed forth
  A putrid cloud above;
And, looked I south, east, west, or north,
  I saw not aught to love.

"I fanned the cheek of brilliant girls,
  And kissed away—their paint!
I danced through many a dandy's curls
  And caught this oily taint.
From offal piles and filthy streets
  One reeking stench arose;
And, mingling with these city sweets,
  The sound of shrieks and blows.

"From every corner hideous men
  Reeled out as they were thrust,
Their mouths afire with rum and gin,
  With blasphemy and lust.
I heard the wife's expiring shriek
  As the wretch drove home the knife,
And saw some things I dare not speak
  In yonder city's life."

The country breeze would hear no more—
  Away the sisters fled:
The wood shook down on each a crown
  Of foliage, brown and red.
And now round some primeval lake,
  O'er hills and pastures bare,
Their freshening flight those breezes take—
  Would I were with them there!

THE OLD BACHELOR'S NEW YEAR.

Oh, the Spring hath less of brightness
Every year,
And the snow a ghastlier whiteness
Every year;
Nor do Summer blossoms quicken,
Nor does Autumn's fruitage thicken
As it did—the seasons sicken
Every year.

It is growing cold and colder
Every year,
And I feel that I am older
Every year;
And my limbs are less elastic,
And my fancy not so plastic,
Yea, my habits grow monastic
Every year.

Tis becoming bleak and bleaker
Every year,
And my hopes are waxing weaker
Every year;
Care I now for merry dancing,

Or for eyes with passion glancing?
Love is less and less entrancing
Every year.

O the days that I have squandered
Every year,
And the friendships rudely sundered
Every year!
Of the ties that might have twined me,
Until time to death resigned me,
My infirmities remind me
Every year.

Sad and sad to look before us
Every year,
With a heavier shadow o'er us
Every year!
To behold each blossom faded,
And to know we might have made it
An immortal garland braided
Round the year.

Many a spectral-beckoning finger,
Year by year,
Chides me that so long I linger,
Year by year;

Every early comrade sleeping
In the churchyard, whither, weeping,
I, alone unwept, am creeping,
Year by year.

SOME WISDOM IN DOGGEREL.

We know not why nor how it is,
Yet find it every hour,
'Twixt Fortune and her sister Mis
There's most unequal power;
How quickly in our noon of pride
May clouds obscure the sun!
How rapidly we fling aside,
The wealth so hardly won!

'Tis so where'er we turn our foot,
And sad it is to write it;
A whole long summer plumps the fruit,—
An hour of frost can blight it!
What are good fortune's thousand smiles

Against her sister's frown?
The ship has sailed a thousand miles—
One shock! she settles down.

'Tis so in love—'tis so in fame—
In all we prize on earth;
The priceless jewel of a name
Untarnished from our birth,
One moment's folly, passion, haste—
The name is ruined,—gone!
So easy 'tis,—so quick we waste
The wealth so hardly won!

Even love—the sweetest flower that stirred
In all life's gloomy vale!
An angry breath, a hasty word,
It sickens in the gale.
O Life! to Death thy hourglass toss,
Let all its sands outrun!
We cannot daily bear the loss
Of joys so dearly won.

THE OPIUM DREAM.

The shadows gather deeper round;
They come with a tumultuous sound
Of muttering thunder,—and they swim
Above me, o'er me, faint and dim—
A thousand forms of speechless dread
Flap on with slow wings o'er my head,
And slowly stooping,—while their eyes
Dilate to an unnatural size,—
Let fall a torchlight, funeral gleam,
Upon their own self-conjured dream.

They come! They sail from darkness out,
A hideous and fantastic rout—
Red eyes in every formless head,
Red clots upon the ghastly dead,
Red robes on every sweltering corse,
Red squadrons, rider, rein and horse,—
They leap from the walls and fill the air,
Their flying garments fan my hair—
God! what an icy touch was there!

Old wrinkled women, in russet clad,
Advancing silently and sad—

Old wrinkled women, whose gleaming eyes
Hint of immortal agonies,
Peeping from under each bodiless hood
Like phosphor sparks in a rotting wood!
Stealthy and silent the beldames all
Creep up the perpendicular wall;
And turning, drop, in my lidless eyes,
Their own unspeakable agonies.

O tide of doubt and utter woe!
Horrible tide, that lies below
The unsounded sea of waking thought!
Dim tide with every monster fraught;
While others, nor more pure nor strong,
Hear in their sleep the seraph's song,
And mount, as ne'er awake they rose,
Superior to terrestrial woes,—
What weird, magnetic spell is thine
That drags me to your hateful brine,
Whene'er my wearied Reason lowers
Her strained hands from the burning oars?

WIDOWOLOGY PHILOSOPHIZED.

I.

Oh, none of your boarding-school misses,
  Your "sweet, timid creatures" for me—
Who rave about Cupid and blisses,
  Yet know not what either may be:
I don't feel at all sentimental,
  Nor care I for Byron a rap,—
But give me a jolly and gentle
  Young widow in weeds and a cap!

II.

To her I would offer my duty,
  For, in truth, all belief it exceeds,
To find how the blossom of beauty
  Is heightened by peeping from "weeds;"—
She is armed *cap-à-pie* for the struggle,—
  To her cap I a captive belong,
And the wink of her magical ogle
  Is a challenge to courtship and song.

III.

The tremors of girlhood are over,
  Love's blossom has ripened to fruit;

And her "first love," asleep under clover,
  Is the soil where my passion takes root:
'Tis pleasant to know, "the departed
  Was tenderly cared to the last"—
And that she will not die broken-hearted,
  If I should pop off just as fast.

IV.

Her temper is never so restive,
  Her duty she knows—and a shape
Is never so sweetly suggestive
  As when it is muffled in crape.
The maid wears one ring when she marries,
  In proof she all others discards—
But the widow-wife wiselier carries
  A pair of these marital guards!

V.

So none of your boarding-school misses,
  Your sweet, timid creatures for me,
Who rave about Cupid and blisses,
  Yet know not what either may be!
I don't feel at all sentimental,
  Nor care I for Byron a rap—
Give me a plump, jolly and gentle
  Young widow in weeds and a cap!

THE WELL-DRESSED MAN.

My poor old coat ! my holy coat !
  But not like that of Treves—
With pain ineffable I note
  Your soiled and tattered sleeves ;
Time was, my coat, that I in you
  Right daintily began
To take of life a jovial view—
  I was a well-dressed man.

My laundress called,—her pay required,—
  I paid—my morning call ;
Attired in thee 'till fairly tired
  I danced at rout and ball :—
The ladies smiled, and as I passed
  The pleasing whisper ran
" There's Mr. H.,—he's rather fast,
  But such a well-dressed man !"

My tailor's bill was much behind,
  And I for board was bored ;
But still the landlady was kind,
  And still mein schneider scored ;—

" He feared to press, but could I pay ?"
'Twas thus the rogue began—
She " really could not turn away
So sweetly dressed a man."

I drove abroad, I drank my wine,—
Match-making mothers sought me,—
And many a maiden fair and fine
Flushed red to think she'd caught me;
With tongue and pen I played my part,
To dazzle was my plan,—
None e'er could deem an aching heart
In such a well-dressed man.

But ah ! it is the utmost pound
That kills the patient camel,—
And to my horror soon I found
My debts I could not trammel;
My tailor's " tick" grew short,—and quick
A hundred duns began—
One suit of clothes had saved their suits
Against the well-dressed man.

I'm beggared now,—but you'll allow
It was a sad temptation.

Obscure to live, while clothes can give
  Respect and social station.
It could not last, my folly's past,
  I've learned a wiser plan,—
By hand and brain I'll be again
  A (paid for) well-dressed man!

WOMAN'S RIGHTS.

I.

O ladies, will you hear a truth,
  Of late too seldom told to you?
Nor deem—he begs it of your ruth—
  The writer over-bold to you.
For, by the pulses of his youth,
  He never yet was cold to you.
And, therefore, 'tis in sober sooth,
  That he would now unfold to you
What may,—apart from rhythmic flights,—
Be called, the sum of "Woman's Rights."

II.

For you the calm sequestered bowers,
  For us to kneel and sue to you;
Your feet upon the path of flowers
  We struggle still to strew to you;
For you to drop the healing showers
  Of kindness, (gentle dew to you,)
On failing health and wasted powers—
  The task is nothing new to you.
"Oh, these, indeed!"—'tis Love indites,—
"These are unquestioned Woman's Rights."

III.

All hail! we cry, the stormiest hours,
  If thus a joy we woo to you!
For us, of life's drugged bowl, the sours,
  If so the sweets ensue to you!
When many a heavy hap was ours,
  Fond retrospection flew to you—
Good husbands and unstinted dowers,
  And smiling babes accrue to you!
And, let me ask, what maiden slights
These latter-mentioned "Woman's Rights?"

IV.

The faithfulness, the grace, the high
  Pure thoughts of life we gain by you;
The vision of a softer eye,
  The finer touch attain by you.
Weak hopes that unto death are nigh
  Outleaning, we sustain by you;
And when misfortune sweeps the sky,
  Our anchored hearts remain by you.
Long days of toil and feverish nights,
Would ill repay these "Woman's Rights."

IV.

When mildewed spinsters, in the sere
  And fruitless leaf, proclaim to you
That "If you knew your 'wrongs' as clear
  As they your 'rights' could name to you—
The tiger, wounded by a spear,
  Would be a creature tame to you,
While tyrant man, in guilty fear,
  Would bow his head in shame to you,"
Reply, "Sour grapes!" and quench the "Lights"
Of this new creed in "Woman's Rights."

VI.

Why quit the calm and holy hearth,
  That is Heaven's antepast to us,
To face the sterner scenes of earth—
  The troubles that are cast to us?
Why change your soul's unsullied mirth
  For woes that rush so fast to us
That we would daily curse our birth,
  Were not your sphere at last to us,—
That sphere of home, which well requites
The loss of these Un-sexing Rights.

THE ISLANDS THAT AWAIT US.

Come, brothers, fill! To-night we will
  Give joy its longest tether,
Take hands around—let music sound—
  We're exiles here together.
For Fatherland we draw the brand,
  We failed, but do not falter;

Some other day again we may
  Fling fire on Freedom's altar.
The toast to-night is one of light,
  Let's drink ere time belate us,
Come, brim the glass and let it pass—
  "The islands that await us!"

There's Cuba lies in sunniest skies,
  By Spanish thraldom trampled;
Her treasure spent, and blood besprent,
  Her wrongs are unexampled.
But exiled sons with Yankee guns
  Can make the tyrants vanish;
For once we'll teach these grandees each
  The way to "walk it Spanish."
The one Lone Star shall not be far
  From our unspotted cluster!
The Southern Queen shall yet be seen
  Arrayed in northern lustre!

There's Ireland, too—'tis vain to rue
  The doom imprinted on her;
Some day we'll make, or we mistake,
  That very curse her honor.

The green shall spread above the red,
  When Saxon blood is under;
And old John Bull at Liverpool
  Be waked by Yankee thunder!
The "Eastern Queen" in starry sheen
  With her of the Antilles,
The Yankees' banner floating high
  O'er shamrocks and o'er lilies.

Then, brethren, fill—pledge heart and will!
  Our "cause" we'll try and gain, too;
The exile's name shall reach a fame
  No king's could e'er attain to!
In France at first was freedom nursed
  But there, so wild and skittish,
She fell a prey one luckless day
  To Spaniards and the British!
But here with growth surpassing both,
  Majestic is her status,
And to her sod, so help us God!
  We'll bring the "Isles that wait us!"

A CALIFORNIAN DITTY.

When lovely Blousalinda Jones,
  (She always was a gadder,)
Did marry, then I took my bones
  To the Seeraw Neevadder.

My pick it seemed to have a charm,
  So quickly did I pocket
Enough to buy a jolly farm,
  To build a house and stock it!

The gold became my child apace,
  And I did rock its cradle,
And for to clean its yaller face
  I used both pan and ladle.

And day by day the bright sun rolled
  Above a brighter treasure;
And day by day in gathering gold,
  I took a wilder pleasure.

The miners called me "Stingy Sam,"
  Because I played no euchre;
But yet I was not then nor am
  The slave of filthy lucre.

There's no man that can see the heart—
  The bosom has no winder—
Else had they seen, from gold apart,
  The love of Blousalinder.

I vowed revenge against that prig,
  (Her husband he,) Joe Slammers.
(He is a cove as wears a wig,
  Is lame, and squints, and stammers.)

I swore that Mrs. S. some day
  Should envy me prodigious;—
I'd live beside her, and display
  What might have been her riches!

I'd lend her husband money, and
  I then would prosecute him:
Were he in that auriferous land
  'Twould be no sin to shoot him.

For this it was I drove my stakes
  Away on Feather river,
(Lord! but I had the ager shakes,
  And suffered from my liver!)

And so, with forty thousand clear,
  I shipped among the sailors:
One April day I landed here,
  And went into a tailor's.

I told him that I wanted all
  My clothes of brightest colors—
The largest patterns (nothing "small,")
  They cost me eighty dollars.

With watches and with golden chains,
  And rings upon my fingers,
I roamed, as do upon the plains
  Them gaudy birds—flamingers.

I started off, as luck did hap,
  To see my Blousalinder—
I saw her in a widow's cap,
  A-sitting at the winder!

She told me that her husband, Joe,
  The very morn of marriage,
Had tripped and broke his precious neck
  A-getting in the carriage;

And how, although she bid me go
    When the night was dark and clammy,
She always loved me more than Joe,
    And then she called me "Sammy!"

IGDRASIL.

The tree of life, that shone so fair
    In Spring's alternate shine and shower,
What bitter fruit its branches bear!
    How soon 'tis stripped of leaf and flower!
As if athwart the sheltering glade
    Had swept the pestilent simoom;
Nor ever more beneath its shade
    Shall violet ope, or primrose bloom!

No more beneath its spreading leaves,
    Shall weary lambs at noontide throng,
While overhead the linnet weaves
    The silken tenor of his song!

No more the pale and sorrowing moon
  Her dewy tears above it weep!
No more at night's unbroken noon
  Shall Muse beneath its branches sleep!

For blight hath fallen on bud and leaf,
  And turned its fruitful sap to gall;
And mildewed in the showers of grief,
  It totters to an early fall!
The bough the redbreast used to love,
  Now nightly hears the owlet hoot—
The locust gnaws the leaves above,
  The cankerworm is at the root!

Then shall it fall, and leave behind
  No record of the brighter past,—
Uprooted by the idle wind,
  And whirled away upon the blast!
Forfend it, Heaven! a soil too warm
  Hath nursed this plague—transplant it now
Where drifting rain and eddying storm,
  May purge the root, and cleanse the bough.

And Hope—who long had listened mute—
  Now raised her azure eyes, and smiled:
She whispered low of future fruit,

And pointed to the distant wild.
Oh, bear it thither! trust in God!
Have faith in my prophetic words,
Again 'twill spread its arms abroad
And shelter its deserted birds!

THE BACHELOR'S ADIEU.

I.

Adieu to the glory of bachelor parties,
The looseness of riot, the cards and the cup!
Old Hymen has caught me—so, farewell! my hearties,
The game (as we say in the vulgate) is up!
No more shall my voice, when 'tis mellowed by sherry,
Troll out the wild glee of the "Grape and the Boar;"
Henceforward, without me, be social and merry—
My voice shall be heard in your circle no more.

II.

Yet sometimes, when Joy her white curtain is flinging
  Between your rapt eyes and the blackness of Care,—
When gaming, and dancing, and drinking and singing
  Usurp the bronze throne of the giant Despair,—
Let memory paint me as once, in your middle,
  I brimmed a full glass to the toast of "The Fair!"
When with trumpet and gong, the cornopian and fiddle,
  We made the dull folk of our neighborhood stare!

III.

O, think of me then; and imagine me sitting,
  "My lip," as she says, "by cigars undefiled,"
Calmly holding a skein for my wife, who is knitting,
  Or rocking a cradle, or dandling a child.
Imagine me thus! and affection will offer
  A tear for the fate of a brother in woe;
Though of Hymen I once was an infidel scoffer,
  He has treated me thus, and will treat you all so.

IV.

Avoid him! For he like a lion is waiting,
  To fall on the careless who saunter along!
He sends a young Cupid, who, laughing and prating,
  Decoys us away with a smile and a song;

He leads up a path that is bordered with roses,
Where sculpture, and grottos, and fountains are rife;
At the end of the vista a Venus reposes;
We kiss her,—and Hymen has noosed us for life!

V.

Henceforward, the fair one whose mystical beauty
Entranced every fibre, and thrilled every bone,
Is ours by the law; and our business and duty
Becomes to love her, and to love her alone!
But ah! to the heart so abhorrent is bondage,
It hates, because right, what 'twould love were it wrong,—
And the path—all so green in our youth and our fond age—
Grows thorny, and tedious, and dreary, and long!

VI.

I'm married, alas! and (of course!) I am happy;
The married (O Lord!) they must "all happy be"—
But I think of the nights when we "bowsed at the nappy,"
And drop a few tears in my third cup of tea.

No more shall the polka's bewild'ring gyrations
  Inflame the warm eyes till they sparkle with love;
I must sit down sedately, and shun such temptations,
  With my thoughts, or my eyes at least, fastened
    above!

VII.

And don't, if you call—Oh, for my sake, remember—
  Don't whisper a word of the nights we have had!
Declare I was always as cold as December,—
  A youth much religious, and gentle and sad,
A man who detested all noise and confusion,
  Who cried that a polka was flagrant and vain,
And would never permit even the slightest infusion
  Of brandy or wine the pure element stain!

VIII.

Above all—not a word of the girl of the ballet
  You found in my rooms when you called rather late
Never venture a hint of Maria or Sally—
  Be silent, in mercy—and "mum" about Kate!
But tell her I loved still to linger and daudle
  The whole evening long o'er religion and tea;
Describe me a pattern young man, and a model
  Of all that a husband should properly be!

THE CRYSTAL PALACE.

Ho! ye who urge the fiery car,
And ye who shoot the flashing spindle,
If labor be prolonged too far,
Both mind and body dwindle!
And ye, who from the stubborn soil
Extort the full of Plenty's chalice,
Come, see the garland woven for Toil,—
Attend the Crystal Palace!

Here men of every clime and line
As brethren meet—as freemen mingle—
And help to deck the industrial shrine
With heart and purpose single.
To lead no martial tilt to-day
Are all these hundred flags unfurled;
Nor meet for internecine fray
The craftsmen of the world.

The central dome—behold it soar,
A kind of glass and iron bubble,
All painted and emblazoned o'er
With much artistic trouble.

And borne on reed-like pillars—dim
  With softened light and rich with gilding
The trellised galleries seem to swim
  Around the liquid building.

Here through the long-resounding aisles,
  The organ's solemn tone is pealing;
And here Italia's sculpture smiles
  In all its wealth of feeling.
Here bright brocades and silks unrolled,
  Around each frescoed column cluster;
And silver groups and cups of gold
  Flash back the noontide lustre.

Here steel-clad knights look wondering down
  On this five-century-later-revel;
They hope to see at least one Crown
  Disturb the vulgar level.
But in the centre—raise your glance!
  That mighty form—we bow before it—
Plucked down the "cap of maintenance"
  And placed the people's o'er it!

O God! 'tis sweet to think there is—
While Europe seems to nerve her sinews
For the last desperate strife—in this
A land where Peace continues.
Transplanted here, on plain and crag
May bloom each flower that Wrong had blighted,
While, awed before our roving flag,
The despot shrinks affrighted!

But why discourse of sober themes?
No intellectual Maine laws bind us,
And we may tipple heavenly dreams
And leave "dull care behind us."
Amid these throngs are young and old—
The gay, the great—a flood of faces;
A clash of tongues—the fair, the bold—
Each with distinctive traces.

The eye is fed on forms of power,
Retained in memory ever after;
The ear drinks music hour by hour,
The hum of speech and laughter.

And, like a hot-house plant, the mind
  Expanding near this crystal fountain
Attains a growth it ne'er may find
  Upon the hermit-mountain.

Man is gregarious; each can strike
  But one chord by his own exertion,
Dipt in Life's sea, Achilles-like,
  We profit by immersion:
And from a myriad bosoms, rife
  With love, one general chorus fleeing,
Bears up to God "The Psalm of Life,"
  The melody of Being.

Then workers from whatever land,
  Of every race and rank, come hither!
And eye to eye, and hand to hand,
  Compare your works together!
Here Art and Toil and Science sit,
  Presiding o'er their mingled treasure;
The feast is spread, sit down to it
  For profit and for pleasure.

THE MORNING SERENADE.

[Translated from Béranger.]

"VIENS AUX CHAMPS."

Rose! the red sun peeps o'er the hill;
 O, quit your couch's soft retreat!
Dost thou not hear the village bell
 Chime forth the hour when we should meet?
The crowded town no pleasure yields,
 Then hie with me—O, hie away!
And, wandering through the flowery fields,
 Let's pass in love the summer's day.

Come, Rose! the fields with flowers are crowned;
 My arm thy gentle prop shall be—
With loving nature all around,
 We too will love more tenderly!
The woodbine bower the linnet shields,
 And there it sings the livelong day;
Then, haste! O, haste then to the fields,
 Where hours, like moments, glide away!

In rustic form our life to mould,
  We'll rise when dawn's first glances peep;
And evening's shadows on the wold
  Shall herald our untroubled sleep;
Perchance to thee this prospect yields
  But tedious days, and weary hours;
Or dost thou love the scented fields,
  The song-birds, and the breezy bowers?

She comes!—the town no more appears—
  O hateful city, fare thee well!
Where art its lifeless beauty rears,
  But genuine passion dare not dwell.
Rose, let us quit Parisian noise,
  For sweet seclusion, far away:
Our moments crowned with rustic joys,
  Our love increasing day by day.

ROMANCE AND ECHO.

I.

It rains, it rains—the slimy street
Is silent, though a hundred feet
In eager hurry homeward beat—
(Coz why? they all wear rubbers.)
They hurry homeward, there to meet
The tender ones who long to greet
Papa and husband—oh! 'tis sweet—
(Wife scolds and baby blubbers.)

II.

The skies have all their clouds amassed,
But sunshine waits them, and will last
When they into their homes have passed:
(I wouldn't like to risk it.)
No rain-tears there, no cutting blast
Of angry words; the hours as fast
As moments fly. They find at last—
(Weak tea and leathern biscuit.)

III.

What tongue describe, what pen portray,
The transports which, at close of day,
The working head and hand repay?
(Due bills, sour looks and twaddle.)
O Seraphina! soon I pray,
With thee to bless my onward way,
Our home, though humble, shall be gay—
(There was a man called "Caudle.")

IV.

I do not smoke—was never "tight"—
And while your beauties charm my sight
I'll find the marriage burden light—
(As soldiers find their knapsacks.)
And home returning night by night,
Your eyes, the hearth, and all things bright,
O, will you not my toils requite,
(With pickled pork and flapjacks?)

"FLEUVE DU TAGE."

[Translated from the French.]

Thou bounding river,
I fly thy tranquil shore.
Farewell! O, never
Shall I behold thee more.
Ye rocks, ye woods, that quiver
To echo's plaintive cry,
Farewell, for ever!
We part and part for aye.

Thou shady grotto!
In raptures deep and true,
When near to Mary
How quick the moments flew!
Thy dark retreat, all lonely,
Where mystery ever dwells,
Was to me, only
Full of delicious spells!

Days when we are glad,
Ye fleet away like dreams!
Days when we are sad,
O, howlong each seems!

Far from my own loved Mary
  For ever severed wide,
Dark, dark, and dreary
  Time rolls its sullen tide !

O valley fairest !
  Sweet valley of my youth !
O Mary, dearest,
  Thee have I loved in truth !
Ye rocks, ye woods that quiver
  To echo's plaintive cry,
Farewell, for ever !
  We part and part for aye !

WHY LOVE THE TURK AND HATE THE CZAR ?

I.

Why should we love the heathen Turk
  And hate the Christian Czar—
While Russia is, in wealth and work,
  " More civilized" by far ?

Her banner bears the Holy Cross
  Wherewith our creed is signed,
While Turkey's Pachas only toss
  Their horsetails to the wind.

II.

Why hate the Czar, and pray for him
  Whose grim seraglio walls
Hold beauties that are growing dim,—
  His concubines and thralls ?
Why hate the Czar and wish success
  To one who dares to libel
Our telegraph and printing press,
  Our cotton goods and Bible ?

III.

The Czar is " civilized,"—of course,—
  He writes it on his banner ;
A Christian praying till he's hoarse
  In the devoutest manner ;
One wife alone he has to kiss,
  As in Church members seemly,—
And in his walk of life he is
  " Respectable extremely."

IV.

The Sultan hath a stud of wives,
And Sultans have—they tell us—
An awkward trick of taking lives
From all obnoxious fellows.
Their headlong passions will not brook
To mingle farce with fury,
And wring from death the killing joke
Of "Murder done by Jury."

V.

The "March of Intellect" is quite
A march beyond their drilling;
They never made a "proselyte"
By one judicious shilling—
Deficient much in legal skill
And "organized starvation,"
They never mixed a patent pill
For Turkish "melioration."

VI.

In fact, we say—with deep regret,
But truth must be our sure hope—
The Sultan is some ages yet
Behind the kings of Europe.

He has not got the royal blood
  Which festers so "divinely"
In men not made of common mud,
  But "porcelain painted finely."

VII.

He has not got the Russian knout
  Wherewith the nuns were beaten;
Nor Austria's axe—grown fat, no doubt,
  On all the flesh it has eaten.
No guilt-extracting guillotine,
  As France has got to cure hers—
But worst of all and deadliest sin,
  He has no "British Jurors."

VIII.

He thinks kings should, against all taste,
  Have nothing underhand meant;
Whereas all know the crown is placed
  Above the tenth commandment.
For we believe that monarchs are
  Exempt from keeping promise;
Especially the Queen and Czar—
  God keep their armies from us!

IX.

Then why, we ask—what mysteries lurk
  That we are so excited,
While burglar Nick and goodman Turk
  Are getting matters righted ?
A friend suggests some twaddling cant
  Of justice and humanity !
Such trifles ought not, and they shan't
  Impede our Christianity.

X.

We want to save the Turkish souls
  By cleaving skulls asunder,—
Destroy them as we did the Poles,
  And profit by the plunder.
We mean to give them gospel light,
  By piercing lights and livers—
When dead and at the judgment-seat,
  They'll then be " true believers !"

XI.

But if—with merely human hearts—
  We ask, " How goes the war ?"
One hoarse-tongued execration starts
  Against the butcher Czar.

There reeks a cloud from Poland's sod,
  That takes a giant form—
A mangled, but immortal god!
  Much wasted, but yet warm.

XII.

And from the plains of Hungary
  Another cloud ascends:
Heaven! what a fury-frenzied eye
  Upon the North it bends.
A woman form—a Juno shape—
  Queen mother of the gods!
A woman, but her shoulders drip
  Ploughed red with Russian rods!

XIII.

Lo! watch them—watch them evermore
  Until the rite be done;
High up in air their lips converge—
  That kiss hath made them one!
From that embrace they quickly turn,
  Their cloud-hands moving north,
And in their eyes the lightnings burn
  Which soon shall thunder forth.

XIV.

God speed the union, sealed in blood,
  Of Freedom and Despair!
God speed the cause of human right
  Whenever and where'er!
God speed the Turk! God speed the Pole!
  God speed whoe'er will fight
With sword and word, heart, brain and hand,
  For man's eternal right!

DUET FOR THE BREAKFAST TABLE.

Romantic Husband—

Thou art my love!—I have none other
  But only thee,—but only thee—

Sensible Wife—

Now Charles, do stop this silly bother;
  And drink your tea,—your cooling tea!

Romantic Husband—

Your eyes are diamonds,—gems refined,—
Your teeth are pearl,—your hair is gold,—

Sensible Wife—

O nonsense now!—I know you'll find
Your cutlets cold,—exceeding cold.

Romantic Husband—

Where'er thou art, my passions burn;
I envy not the monarch's crown!

Sensible Wife—

Put some hot water in the urn,
And toast this bread, and toast it brown!

Romantic Husband—

Had I Golconda's wealth, I say,
'Twere thine at will, 'twere thine at will;

Sensible Wife—

Then let me have a check to pay
The dry-goods bill,—that tedious bill!

Romantic Husband—

O heed it not, my trembling flower!—
If want should press us, let it come!

Sensible Wife—

And, apropos, the bill for flour
Is quite a sum,—an unpaid sum.

Romantic Husband—

So rich in love—so rich in joy—
No change our cup of bliss can spill.

Sensible Wife—

Now do be quiet:—you destroy
My cambric frill,—my well-starched frill.

Romantic Husband—

Ha! senseless, soulless, loveless girl,
To sympathy and passion dead!

Sensible Wife—

A moment since I was your "pearl,"
Your "only love"—at least, you said.

Romantic Husband—

I spoke it in the bitter jest
Of one his own deep sadness scorning.

Sensible Wife—

Well, candor is at all times best;
I wish you, sir, a fair good morning!

THE PRISONER OF WAR.

[Translated from Béranger.]

LES HIRONDELLES.

A captive on Africa's shore,
A warrior laden with chains,
Exclaimed—I behold ye once more,
As ye fly from the frozen plains,

Ye swallows, whom Hope, in despite
  Of this fierce-glowing climate, pursues !—
From France ye have taken your flight—
  Of my home do ye bring me no news ?

Three summers, I've begged that ye might
  Recall the fond wishes that stray
To that vale, where in dreams of delight,
  My youth rolled unheeded away—
To the river whose winding waves foam
  'Neath lilac bowers, scenting the breeze !
Ye have perched on my sweet cottage-home—
  Have ye nothing to tell me of these ?

Perchance your young nestlings were born
  'Neath the roof where I welcomed the day !
Ye have pitied my mother's heart torn
  By the love which can never decay !
Though dying she hopes that each hour
  My step on the silence will break—
She listens—and fast her tears shower,—
  Of her love have ye nothing to speak ?

My sister! perchance she is wed!
  Have ye seen the gay youth who in throngs
At the feast of her bridal were met,
  And welcomed her marriage with songs?
And those—my companions of yore—
  Who lived through the combats we fought—
Do they dwell in the village once more?
  Of so many friends know ye naught?

It may be the stranger's foot presses
  The graves in the vale where they sleep!
My home a new master possesses—
  He causes my sister to weep;
No prayers that for me wing to Heaven,
  And torture and fetters below—
Your silence in mercy is given
  To spare me this burden of wo?

MATRIMONIAL COMPLACENCY.

Since Grace and I were double,
  I'd have the world to know,
We've been a goodish couple,
  As goodish couples go!
To no ecstatic passion
  Our present hearts respond;
But it is out of fashion
  For couples to be fond.

She is not quite a "seraph,"
  A "being born above,"—
As milliner and sheriff
  With bills and writs can prove;
Her dress is more than costly,
  Her taste in music fine—
She eats, and it is vastly
  As other people dine.

I thought her once angelic—
  A fairy she did seem;
There is not now a relic
  Of that diviner dream.

She don't object to heaping
  A pie-plate filled before;
And once, when she was sleeping,
  I thought I heard a snore!

Nor am I now her hero,
  The "worshipped one alone;"
A matrimonial Nero
  She seems to think me grown.
"A brute," should I refuse her
  That "dear, sweet Cashmere shawl"—
"Worse than a brute I use her,"
  If kept in town the fall.

Cigars are her "abhorrence,"
  She "hates the sight of wine,"
And "no presumption warrants"
  A friend brought home to dine;
She won't believe 'tis business
  That keeps me late at night,—
And on the slightest dizziness,
  I am condemned as "tight"

But still, despite this trouble,
  These little puffs of woe,
We make a goodish couple,
  As goodish couples go!

To no ecstatic passion
 Our present hearts respond;
But it is out fashion
 For couples to be fond.

WE MIGHT HAVE BEEN.

There is a whisper ringing clear
In every sleepless listener's ear,
A whisper of but scanty cheer,
And heard distinctlier every year—
 " You might have been—you might have been."

Breathing throughout the hush of night,
It shuns companionship and light;
A knell, a blessing, and a blight,
We profit if we hear aright
 " You might have been—you might have been."

As memory bids the past arise,
The soaring hopes that swept the skies,
(Each in its narrow grave now lies,)
We hear, and not with tearless eyes,
  " You might have been—you might have been."

We might have won the meed of fame,
Essayed and reached a worthier aim—
Had more of joy and less of shame,
Nor heard, as from a tongue of flame,
  " You might have been—you might have been."

SOME TALK ABOUT POETS.

LAURA.

Do tell me what's a Poet, ma?
  I'm sure I meant to please him,
But when this morn I asked papa,
  He told me not to tease him!
And so does every one I ask
  So (of course) I long to know it,
It can't be such a mighty task
  To tell one what's a Poet

MAMMA.

You silly girl!—why, how absurd
To ask papa that question!
I'm sure it was your very word
That spoiled his day's digestion!
My dear, they're men who've long annoyed
All good and prudent mothers,
They're men, my love, you must avoid
As much as younger brothers!

LAURA.

But why, mamma? You said, be sure,
And still this precept carry,
That younger sons are always poor,
And very seldom marry.
But what on earth have poets done,
That we should scorn and scout 'em?
And there's Letitia Vane, for one,
I know is crazed about 'em!

MAMMA.

Then, Laura, I may say at once
They must be coldly treated!
They're poorer even than younger sons,
And dreadfully conceited.

They've little gold, except it be
  The gilding on their covers,
And prudent mothers all agree
  They are most dangerous lovers.

THE LAST MOSQUITO.

Thou faintest, last mosquito
  With which my room was rife!
The frost has put a veto
  Upon thy further life.
Though thou wert a backbiter
  When June o'erflushed the sky.
It is not in the writer
  To doom thee now to die.

No more thy horn shall wake us—
  The nights are now too chill;
No longer canst thou make us
  The victims of thy bill;

Our children we love dearly,
  They are our blood and line;
But thou, I know, art nearly
  All flesh and blood of mine.

Alas, thou withering 'skeeter!
  When August yet was fresh,
Perchance thou wast an eater
  Of Laura's roseate flesh!
That flesh of dazzling whiteness,
  Too pure for touch of mine—
The thought even lends a brightness
  To this thy cold decline!

We spread our nets for fishes,
  To drag them in, no doubt;
With thee our only wishes
  Were still to keep thee out;
Full oft from some ecstatic,
  Bright dream recalled, I rose—
And found thee in the attic,
  A-fattening on my nose.

" But life is fleet—how fleet, oh!"
  As Mrs. Norton sings—
And now thou last mosquito
  Dost spread thy withering wings!
Thou hast escaped and battened
  Thus late into the fall;
Thy comrades there lie flattened
  And dead upon the wall.

'Tis thus thy summer passes—
  'Twere well our life so passed,
Sweet flowers, soft arms, full glasses
  Around our pathway cast!
But we must bide the bitter
  Cold winters as they come—
Why, darn the eternal critter,
  He's bit me on the thumb!

SPIRIT RAPPING.

[Some lines on the introduction into the Massachusetts Legislature of a bill for the "Suppression of Spiritual Manifestations."]

"De par le Roi! Defense a Dieu
De faire miracles en ce lieu."

I.

What! pass a statute to dispatch 'em!
It is a proposition rare;
Imprison,—hang—(when you first catch 'em,)
The bodiless spirits of the air!—
Despise all reason,—hear no question,—
The scourge of legal power is thine;
Condemn—and then ('twill aid digestion)
Say "Grace" before you dine!

II.

Of old, when glorious Galileo
Announced the planetary plan,
A Pope,—a sacerdotal Leo,
Declared his doctrine under ban;
But, though the church affirmed his error,
The world has since his truth averred—
And, in despite of condign terror,
The spirits will be heard!

III.

When Franklin raised his brawny arm
  To rob the lightning's callow nest,
(Where little thunder gods did swarm
  Beneath the electric mother's breast :)
Why did no Yankee Pope arise
  To bid the impious hand withdraw,
Spreading an ægis o'er the skies
  Of Massachusetts Law ?

IV.

O Liberty ! thou splendid word,
  We do adore thy claptrap name !
'Tis reverenced wheresoever heard,
  But violated, just the same !
Shall men with narrow brows and hearts
  Forbid our spiritual faith ?
" Rap ! Rap !" from the dull table starts,
  It lends a spur to death !

V.

No ! by the hallowed rights we wrung
  In years of blood from Britain's hand—
No ! by the stars—heaven's cressets !—hung
  In the blue dome that spans our land !

We will not yield to fogy drill,
  We scorn and hate its idiot ban,
With force of intellect and will
  We claim the rights of man.

VI.

The right to hope, the right to pray,
  The right of conscience and of rest,
The right to choose whatever way,
  Unhurting others, suits us best.
We re-affirm in reverent awe
  This heresy that Knox began,
That conscience towers o'er human law,
  That God is more than man!

THE BROKEN HEART.

[From the French.]

Her heart was broken; day by day
She wasted silently away;
And o'er her large dark eyes there grew
A film of leaden-colored hue;
Her step was languid, slow and weak,
A hectic fever flushed her cheek—
Seldom and little did she speak.

And he to whom her faith was vowed,
Her husband—by the world allowed
A kind, good-natured, easy man—
O'er all his present conduct ran
To see if he had given her ought
To cause this apathy of thought—
This tearful silence, sorrow fraught!

At length she spoke one dewy morn—
"Adolphe, you wonder why forlorn
I pensive sit from day to day,
And pine in solitude away.
Dear husband, I will tell thee all:
My neighbor, Madame D'Argental,
Has got—I have not—a new shawl."

THE FIRST OF MAY.

The first of May—the first of May—
What lying poet called it gay?
There is the very deuce to pay,
And no pitch hot, the first of May!

The house I took a twelvemonth since,
And furnished fit to lodge a prince—
That cheerful house I quit to-day,
Because it is the first of May.

My carpets all are torn to shreds,
We have not where to lay our heads;
The beds are all unscrewed, and we
Are screwed as tight as men can be.

Our new piano—new no more—
In fragments lies upon the floor;
Our china service, once so neat,
Now helps to pave the dusty street.

"Alas!" I cry in utter grief,
"Would Heaven I were an Arab chief
He roams about unrented places,
And camps in every green oasis."

The wagoners alone can say
The festival is truly gay;
The scoundrels get a fortnight's pay
For working on the first of May.

THE LAST RESORT.

A dramatist declared he had got
So many people in his plot,
That what do do with half he had
Was like to drive him drama-mad !
" The hero and the heroine
Of course are married—very fine !
But with the others, what to do
Is more than I can tell ; can you?"

His friend replied—" 'Tis hard to say,
But yet I think there is a way.
The married couple thank their stars,
And half the 'others' take the cars ;
The other half you put on board
An Erie steamboat,—take my word,
They'll never trouble you again !"
The dramatist resumed his pen.

THINE EYES OF BLUE.

[From the French.]

Thine eyes of blue,—the heaven's own hue,—
  Thy soft eyes thrill my fevered pulse;
The fire that lies within thine eyes
  Hath blinded me to all things else!

Love at a single word may bloom,
  The full heart blossoms fair and free;
One glance may gild the future's gloom,
  And now thy bright eyes shine on me!
                Thine eyes of blue, &c.

And canst thou ask me why my cheek,
  Where thou art not, grows pale and wan?
Why sadness that I cannot speak
  Surrounds my path when thou art gone?
                Thine eyes of blue, &c.

And further canst thou wish to know
  What change comes o'er me when we meet?
And why my pallid brow will glow,
  And why my quivering pulses beat?

Thine eyes of blue,—the heaven's own hue!
  Thy soft eyes thrill my fevered pulse;
The fire that lies within thine eyes
  Hath blinded me to all things else!

THE THRONE AND THE WORKSHOP.

[Translated from the French.]

I.

While all the arts with trophies bright
  To prove the wide world's wealth combine,
It seems as though some genial sprite
  Had helped to deck the Crystal shrine!

II.

Be England long to fame endeared,
  Who—bidding rival passions cease—
Extends to those she lately feared
  The hand of welcome and of peace!

III.

To all the world a challenge speeds,
  And on her hospitable soil,
To the red strife of war succeeds
  The bloodless tilt of art and toil.

IV.

The lords of labor pile on high
  Their works beneath the shining dome;
And sing no longer "let us die,"
  But "live to bless our native home!"

V.

Our battle-field a palace gay!
  Our victor's robes unstained and white!
The peaceful workman bears away
  The cross of honor from the fight!

VI.

The rich, the learned, the gifted sons
  Of art and labor throng the hall;
A band of brethren, knit at once
  To bless the green earth, free to all!

VII.

Then, courage! Ceaseless toil will bring
  The workshop level with the throne!
And all the titles of a king,
  Be naught to that we laborers own!

THE LAST APPEAL.

Brethren, 'tis the last appeal,
  Of human woe to outraged Heaven!
God witness for us, that we feel
Reluctant all to draw the steel!
  But what hope else to us is given?
  The bonds of social concord riven,
    We try the last appeal!

Brethren, on! one stubborn fight,
  And peace for evermore shall be!
  The Red Sea's waves will soon unite,
Above the vanquished hosts of Might;
  And conquest lead us into thee,
  Sweet Canaan of liberty,
    Where God protects the Right!

Brethren! Power's triumphant heel
Hath struck us oft; but now we turn!
And they who wronged us soon shall feel
The spell that lurks in patriot zeal,
Their bonds to break, their threats to spurn—
The victor's wreath, or martyr's urn,
Await the Last Appeal!

A PUNGENT CONSIDERATION.

I.

Of all the trades that men can call
Unpleasant and offensive,
The Editor's is worst of all,
For he is ever pensive;
His leaders lead to nothing high—
His columns are unstable,
And though the printers make him pi,
It does not suit his table.

II.

The Carpenter,—his course is plane,
His bit is always near him—
He augurs every hour of gain,—
He chisels—and none jeer him.
He shaves, yet is not close, they say,—
The public pay his board, sir,
Full of wise saws, he bores away,
And so he swells his hoard, sir.

III.

St. Crispin's son—the man of shoes,
Has awl things at control, sir;
He waxes wealthy in his views,
But ne'er neglects his sole, sir.
His is indeed a heeling trade,
And when we come to casting
The toetal profits he has made,
We find his ends are lasting.

IV.

The Tailor, too, gives fits to all,
Yet never gets a basting;
His cabbages, however small,
Are most delicious tasting.

His goose is heated—(happy prig!)
  Unstinted is his measure;
He always plays at thimblerig,
  And seams a man of pleasure.

V.

The Farmer reaps a fortune plump,
  Though harrowed far from woe, sir;
His spade for ever proves a trump,
  His book is I've-an-hoe, sir;
However corned, he does not slip,
  Though husky, never hoarse, sir,
And in a plow-share partnership,
  He gets his share of course, sir.

VI.

The Sailor on the giddy mast,
  (Comparatively master,)
Has many a bulwark round him cast
  To wave away disaster.
Even shrouds to him are full of life,
  His mainstay still is o'er him,
A gallant and top-gallant crew
  Of *beaux esprits* before him.

VII.

The sturdy Irish Laborer picks
  And climbs to fame ;—'tis funny,
He deals with none but regular bricks,
  And so he pockets money.
One friend sticks to him,—(mortar 'tis),—
  In hodden gray, unbaffled,
He leaves below an honest name
  When he ascends the scaffold.

VIII.

The Printer, though his case be hard,
  Yet sticks not at his hap, sir ;
'Tis his to canonize the bard,
  And trim a Roman cap, sir.
Some go two-forty,—what of that ?
  He goes it by the thousand !
A man of form and fond of fat,
  He loves the song I now send.

IX.

The Engine-driver, if we track
  His outward semblance deeper,
Has got some very tender traits—
  He ne'er disturbs the sleeper.

And when you switch him as he goes,
  He whistles all the louder;
And should you brake him on the wheel,
  It only makes him prouder.

X.

I launched this skiff of rhyme upon
  The trade-winds of the muses;
Through pungent seas they've borne it on,
  The boat no rudder uses:
So masticate its meaning once,
  And judge not sternly of it—
You'll find a freight of little puns,
  And very little profit.

NEW-YORK CRYSTAL PALACE.

I.

Ye wha direct the Exhibition,
An' manage a' things wi precision,
Mock na a simple bard's petition,
          Wha's pouch is bare,
An' yet wad like to feast his vision
          On yon big Fair.

II.

'Tis true I'm but a poortith wight,
Come here to warstle and to fight,
For roof and hearth, for claes an' bite,
My voice is sma',
But no afeard to crack the right
Afore ye a'.

III.

Though fifty cents be sma' to you,
A mere card-counter, like eneugh,
There's mony an honest lad wad rue
That sma' amount ;
His childrens' bellies maun be fou',
An' trifles count.

IV.

If yon were like a kintra show,
To which but aince we spier to go,
Your bonnie charge, though far frae low,
I wad na shun;
I'd in, and tak the foremost row,
An' see the fun.

V.

But your's is nae sic feckless play
That ane can ken it in a day,
Unless in a bewildered way
He gapes an' glowers;—
Sic wark demands and wad repay
Sax score of hours.

VI.

An' how, I ask, can chiels afford,
Wha's gains are sma', an' labor hard,
A muckle sum that should be shared
Wi' his wee bodies ?
I'm feard they'd lack for bed and board,
An' shoes and duddies.

VII.

For bye, in an industrial tilt,
Though ither flags be bonnier gilt,
Wha's banner should gang first in till't
Unless of those
Wha's joints hae cracked, wha's sweat was spilt,
Afore it rose ?

VIII.

What hae the rich, the dizzened crowd,
In a' the place to mak them proud?
They neither welded, wove, nor plow'd,
Nor bleart their eyne—
Whyles Labor may proclaim aloud,
"The work is mine!

IX.

"Frae deep foundation e'en to dome,
The glit'rin' aisles through which you roam,
The gallery that, light as foam,
Ower a' expands,
The palace and its treasures come
Frae these rough hands!"

X.

Let Sedgwick now (a sonsy man)
Tell the Directors o' his plan,
An' say, "Though wrangly we began,
'Tis time to truckle;
A thousand mickle soon outrun
The five-score muckle."

XI.

Here folk frae ilka clime are met,
A wae-disposed monarchic set,
A' peering round, if they can get
(Lang may they need them!)
Some proofs to say that "Labor yet
Wins nocht frae freedom."

XII.

Ye may despise us, an' ye will,
But we're the men to foot your bill;
The "Upper Ten" hae looked their fill,
An should you flout us,
I'm feard ye'll hae an empty till
At best without us.

XIII.

An' what for no should we na'* rin
(Some points demand it) out an' in?
The stummochs o' us working men
Are easy snarling;
But ower the whirligig we grin
Like Sternie's Starling.

XIV.

Let Sedgwick tak anither thought!
Kickshaws to labor's wame are naught,
Nor can we pay the prices sought
By those bright lasses
Frae whom, mysel' yestreen, I bought
Twa jelly glasses.

XV.

Dupont an' Davis—soldiers baith—
I swear till ye, upon my aith,
That though ye aft hae grappled death,
Wi sabres carvin',
Ye wad na bide the risin' wrath
O' downright starvin'.

XVI.

I'm done;—nor care I now a flee,
If high or low you gar it be;
But this I swear, nae doit frae me
Your nieves shall mortar
Till into yon big house the key
Is "cash—one quarter!"

TRUTH IN PARENTHESIS.

I love—O more than words can tell,
  (Your five-and-thirty thousand shiners,)
You draw me by a nameless spell,
  (As California draws the miners.)
You are so rich in beauty's dower,
  (And rich in several ways beside it,)
Had I your hand within my power,
  (Across a banker's draft to guide it,)
No care my future life could dim—
(My tailor, too! what joy to him!)

O, should you change your name for mine,
  (I've given my name—on bills—to twenty,)
Existence were a dream divine,
  (At least so long as cash was plenty.)
Our home should be a sylvan grot,
  (Bath, billiard, smoking-room and larder,)
And there, forgetting and forgot,
  (My present need I'd live the harder;)
Our days should pass in fresh delights,
(Lethargic days and roaring nights.)

O say, my young, my fawn-like girl,
  (She's old enough to be my mother,)
Let "yes" o'erleap those gates of pearl!
  (My laughter it is hard to smother;)
Let lips that love hath formed for joy,
  (For joy, if they her purse resign me,)
Long hesitate ere they destroy,
  (And to a debtor's jail consign me,)
The heart that beats but to adore
(Yourself the less, your fortune more.)

Consent—consent, my priceless love,
  (Her price is five-and-thirty thousand,)
I swear by all, around, above,
  (Her purse-strings now, I feel, are loosened,)
I have not loved you for your wealth,
  (Nor loved at all, as I'm a sinner;)
O bliss! you yield, one kiss by stealth!
  (I'm sick—that kiss has spoiled my dinner;)
Now early name the blissful day,
(My duns grow clamorous for their pay.)

ORIGIN OF THE HAIR CHAIN.

Love went one day a foolish quest;
He could not rest,
But wandered idly to and fro
In deepest woe
And wrung his hands, as if in pain,
And cried "A chain!
I need a subtle chain to bind,
A captive mind!
A captive heart I seek to bind,
Yet thrall nor bonds nor fetters find!"

Old Hymen hobbled from the church,
And in the porch,
Cried, "Hither! I have chains to sell
Will please you well!
Once bound in my law-hallowed chain
None ever gain,
Except by death, their liberty!
Step in and see
The spells o'er which I glibly run
To bind two faithful hearts in one!"

"Your spells are vain!" the god replied,
"They have been tried;
I need an ever-during thrall,
Not one to gall!
You bind the purse—you bind the hand,
In ceaseless band!
The thoughts, affections, all I try
To knit for aye,
You cannot bind. I would rather lose
My captive, than such bondage use!"

Then Venus came, and found the child
Distraught and wild;
And still he wandered to and fro,
In deepest woe,
And wrung his hands in hopeless pain,
And cried, "A chain!
I need a subtle chain to bind
A captive mind;
A captive heart I seek to bind
Yet thrall, nor bonds, nor fetters find!"

Her dark hair o'er her bosom flowing,
(That bosom glowing
With tenderest thoughts!) the goddess smiled,
And kissed the child.

She stilled his sobs with fond caress,
And chose a tress—
A long dark tress that fell below
Her breast of snow.
"Weave this into a chain my child!"
The urchin kissed her hand and smiled.

And now in young Love's myrtle bower,
For many an hour,
The Graces ply their pleasing task—
And should you ask
What young Love did, he quickly rolled,
Of virgin gold,
A love-knot for the woven chain,
Nor toiled in vain!
For in that glittering bondage ta'en
The captive smiled, and kissed his chain.

MAXIMS OF THE NEWSPAPER.

I.

A paragraph to make one laugh,
Should be of ten lines just a half;
A trivial theme,—a brilliant stream
Of verbiage, metaphor and dream,—
Such as this paragraph I deem!

II.

A stirring song is never long,
But must be fiery, deep and strong;
With much of thought, not fully wrought,
But in dim glimpses shown and caught;
Such are the rules Anacreon taught.

III.

A good critique should ever seek
To check the proud, and help the weak;
Not swayed by fame, nor prone to blame,
Calm, energetic, never tame,
And judging all men just the same.

IV.

A tale or sketch should never fetch
Its hero from thy hand, Jack Ketch;
Though for a time the tide of crime
Roll down white-crested and sublime,
It leaves a track of venomed slime.

V.

In short, be brief!—each added leaf
Is so much to your reader's grief,
The point is gone: the lightning shone
And dies while yet we labor on;
True wit ne'er knows a second dawn!

VI.

Observe these rules, and mock the "Schools
Of composition" taught by fools!
Briefness and wit together flit,
And fly, like Parthians, when they hit—
The urchins are too wise to sit.

ADIEU.

O! heed him not, if poet prate
  Of parted love and endless woe;
  True love would scorn to babble so
And grief is inarticulate;
  Or with a hoarse and broken flow
It rushes, murmuring, to its fate;
That ocean which, or soon or late,
  Receives the wreck of all we know,
Or be it love, or be it hate.
O heed him not! The spirit bowed
With grief like mine was ne'er so loud!

But if to say in simple phrase
  That I will ne'er forget you, friends,
  Though at the earth's remotest ends
I pass my long unsolaced days;
  That when the evening shade descends,
And high and bright the fagots blaze,
My faithful heart your forms shall raise,
  While memory the curtain rends
That time would drop o'er earlier days—
If this content you, 'tis sincere,
Though vouched by neither oath nor tear.

THE CRUSADER SONG.

[From the Russian.]

I.

Before the Holy Image
  I thrice have bent to-night,
And, having paid my orisons,
  Now rush to join the fight—
The fight of faith and fatherland,
  For this I rush afar,
My life and lance for Russia!
  My fealty to the Czar!

II.

My sword—the only heritage
  My valiant fathers left,
Hath bit the flesh of Sweden,
  And many a Tartar cleft;
Too long in shameful idleness
  The rusting blade hath lain,
And now it longs for blood to cleanse
  The dull, corroding stain!

III.

From the summit of the Balkan
  Our brethren stretch their hands;
They pray to us to rescue them—
  Their prayers become commands!
We feel for them, will fight for them,
  For God and us they bleed;
The weaponed strength of Russia goes
  To strike for Russia's creed!

IV.

The memories of our church are twined
  Round Kiew's white-bastioned crest—
The loveliest and the brightest town
  That ever Turk oppressed.

Those memories are consecrate,
  And shadow forth the doom
Which gathers strength in silence,
  And will quickly burst the gloom.

V.

The cross of pain, the spear of might,
  On these our strength we cast;
The hand of God protected both
  In ages long o'erpast.
Think you our hearts so soon forget
  The sires for whom we mourn?
Their sons shall bear the flag of faith
  As it by them was borne.

VI.

We go to break the Moslem's pride,
  To crush his creed accursed—
Then welcome be the Holy War,
  And let its tempest burst!
Be this our victor battle cry,
  As east and south we press—
"The God that blesses Russia,
  And the Czar the Russians bless!"

SONNETS.

ON READING THE "ARABIAN NIGHTS."

Grandest and best of all the motley train
That hail old Fiction as their deathless sire!
How cold beside thy Asiatic fire,
Are all creations of the northern brain!
Dull, leaden pictures of experienced pain,
And pulseless love-tales over which we tire!
Whoso possesseth thee does not require
This world at all—for, on thy page, we gain
A lovelier earth, a loftier life than ours,
Full of good Genii, Mermaids, and the Moon,
Affrites and Fairies, prompt to every boon,
Fountains and gems, and broidered robes and flowers,
And diamond gates that hinge in golden towers,
And love at dewy ease in paradisal bowers!

SUMMER'S DEATH.

The garden flower-stalks, black and pinched with cold,
The wood-path strewn with red and yellow leaves,
And the hoarse murmur which the tempest weaves
Through the bare branches,—as though Autumn told

With groans the agony of growing old
  And dying poor and naked. Nature grieves
  That the brief gleam of sunshine so deceives,
When, for an hour at noon, the clouds unfold
And show the Day-God,—bright, no longer warm,
  Luring each shivering insect coyly forth
  With the glad hope of Summer's second birth,
A hope, alas! soon rifled by the storm!
The birds with shriller note foretell the dearth
Now hovering in the clouds o'er the late smiling earth!

TO HELEN—A POETESS.

We ne'er have met in the world's busy throng,
  And in the world 'tis chance if e'er we meet;
  Yet in the shadow of the woods 'tis sweet,
Even though we know not whence, to hear the song
Of the wild robin, as her notes prolong
  The hymn of joy!—or in the lonely glen,
  Moonlit, and far from the abodes of men,
To list the streamlet as it chafes along
  Its bright and winding course thro' summer flowers,
Old moss-grown rocks and interlacing roots,
Where scarce a ray through the thick foliage shoots

Down to the tide, and the entangled bowers
Of sedge and lily! Thus entranced I hear
The minstrel still unknown, her utterance sweet and
clear.

TO BENJAMIN B. SHILLABER.

(A Moon Sonnet.)

Around the sun the earth has but half sped
Since first I saw thee; yet it almost seems
As if I must have met thee in the dreams
That long ago ran riot through my head.
If all were true Pythagoras once said,
Then would I say,—In yon fair planet's beams
Our souls had mingled like two kindred streams,
And parted thence, in different channels led,
Down to this ocean of the present earth;
You in New England first, and elsewhere I,
Leaped out of darkness, and beheld the sky,
Through the thick vapors of our human birth;
Then,—by some hidden sympathy controlled,
Our streams of life converged, and were together
rolled!

TO A LADY EDITOR.

Welcome, dear Helen, to the reverend chair,
From which we pen these rhapsodies of ours!
Though not so lovely as the muses' bowers,
Nor quite exempted from life's wear and tear,
(As every earthly rose a thorn must bear!)
Still let us hope that you will find the flowers
More thickly scattered. On the loftiest towers
The storm strikes fiercest; but a purer air
Plays round the pinnacle; and standing there,
A wider landscape animates our powers,
Sun-bright, and green, and freshened by the showers,
A larger life and wider view we share!
Heaven's breath, if keen, is pure; and they who dare
The empyrean height avoid the low-born fogs of care.

TO A FOUNTAIN

That played only during the daytime in summer.

Green-wooded fountain! with how glad a rush
Thou leapest up from the surrounding clay,
Cleaving toward heaven thy rainbow-colored way,
And gleaming brightly in the crimson flush
Spread o'er the west. Anon, the starry hush
Of night will lull thee, and thy drifted spray
No more shall fall, like an alighting fay,

On the dry leaves now revelling in thy gush !
Say, friends, if love's rich fountain e'er shall fail
To fling its freshening waters from the heart,
In sorrow's night shall its loud tide depart,
And its bright plumage cease to fan the gale ?
Shall we who shared its noontide ever know
That Love, like it, alas ! has but a summer flow ?

SPIRITUAL MANIFESTATIONS.

It seems as if the veil were rent atwain
Which hid the future from the present world ;
While from the deep abyss before are hurled
Swift beams of light into this waste of pain
Which men call life. It may be that in vain
We hear the spirit voices of the past
Rise out of chaos, tremulous and fast,
To fall on the sick soul like summer rain.
But, if delusion, it is yet so sweet
To think the perished live in higher spheres
And share with us our earthly hopes and fears,
That I, for one, will cherish the deceit,
And say to those who chide me for my faith—
Peace for a few short years ! all will be known in death.

THE BACCHANTE.

Say, art thou sad?—my golden cup
  With precious balm is laden;
A world of joy in every drop,
  For man, and, eke, for maiden.
Its scent outvies the rosy ties
  That in my tresses cluster;
The light that lies within mine eyes
  Grows pale beside its lustre!

My zone ungirt, my bosom warm,
  My thoughts at random roaming—
Wilt thou refuse the fragrant charm?
  Wilt thou refuse it foaming?
Its scent outvies the rosy ties
  That in my tresses cluster;
The light that lies within mine eyes
  Grows pale beside its lustre!

THE MINER'S DREAM.

I lie, all cold and lonely,
Beneath an elm at night,
When the stars are shining only
And the glowworm twinkles bright;
I sleep where the star-gleams quiver,
And my restless memories roam
Away from the golden river,
To my boyhood's happy home!

The golden dream is fleeting
Away from my troubled sight,
And my heart with hope is beating,
As I see the cottage light;
My father's cot before me,
Where in bygone hours I dwelt,
Ere the clouds of life came o'er me,
When no pain my bosom felt.

I see my mother smiling,
With a faint, uneasy mirth,
And my father's hands are piling
The fagots on the hearth;

And they whisper ever lowly,
  And I think I hear my name—
It was breathed in accents holy,
  And a teardrop with it came!

The golden sands are gleaming
  In the ruddy flush of dawn,
The golden sun is beaming,
  And my nightly dream is gone;
But ever and for ever
  In my sleep my wild thoughts roam
Away from the golden river,
  To my boyhood's happy home!

ALAS, THEY MET!

Alas! they met ere life had lost
  One tinge of summer's ruddy morn!
Ere yet a cloud their heaven had crossed,
  Ere yet their path had known a thorn!
And, hand in hand, they wandered on,
  Or stayed but to collect the flowers,
Love's light o'er all the future shone,
  And Pleasure led the smiling hours!

O, well for them if from that dream
  Of bliss their spirits ne'er had woken!
If they had sunk beneath the stream
  Of life, that heavenly trance unbroken!
They should have died ere sorrow came,
  In Death's dark house, as here, united,
And quitted earth ere sin or shame
  One leaf of Love's pure wreath had blighted!

FEMININE ARITHMETIC.

[A very old "Joe."]

LAURA.

On me he shall ne'er put a ring,
  So, mamma, 'tis in vain to take trouble—
For I was but eighteen in spring,
  While his age exactly is double.

MAMMA.

He's but in his thirty-sixth year,
  Tall, handsome, good-natured and witty,
And should you refuse him, my dear,
  May you die an old maid without pity!

LAURA.

His figure, I grant you, will pass,
And at present he's young enough plenty;
But when I am sixty, alas!
Will not he be a hundred and twenty?

ROMEO AND JULIET.

JULIET.

One kiss before you go, love,
One kiss before we part!
Indeed, you do not know, love,
The sadness of my heart!
The dawn that wakes the birds, love,
To joy, is pain to me!
I hear your farewell words, love,
Nor care how bright it be!

Oh! softly down the stream, love,
Let your light oars be driven;
For I have dreamt a dream, love,
Perchance a warning given;

I dreamt my brother stood, love,
And saw our parting kiss
It cannot bode us good, love,
Be sure, forget not this!

Nor must thou yet forget, love,
At night-fall to return,
When o'er the parapet, love,
You see the signal burn;
Adieu! we may not stay, love,
Cease not to think of me!
And through the weary day, love,
I'll pray for night and thee.

ROMEO.

O hush! your fears are vain, love,
Nor sire, nor brother near,
Indeed I may remain, love,
There is no danger here!
The prying dawn delays, love,
As loth to break our bliss,
He did but peep to win from thee,
The fond, the parting kiss!

The willows, bending deep, love,
  In prudent awe look down,
They will not raise their heads to peep,
  Lest you, my love, should frown;
The birds are all asleep, love,
  Oh, chide not my delay!
For where thou art not is my night—
  Where'er thou art my day.

Alas! the spell is riven, love,
  I hear the bells afar,
Dost thou not see in heaven, love,
  Yon dimly fading star?
When in the dewy eve, love,
  It rises o'er the hill,
You'll see my shallop on the stream
  And hear my bugle shrill.

Adieu! It is the dawn, love,
  I must—I must away!
The fading star hath gone, love,
  The birds awake the day:
To part at all is pain, love,
  To thee and me, I wis,
But till we meet again, love,
  O, keep my parting kiss!

THE MUSHROOM HUNT.

In early days, ere Common Sense
  And Genius had in anger parted,
They made to friendship some pretence,
  Though each, Heaven knows ! diversely hearted.
To hunt for mushrooms once they went,
  Through nibbled sheepwalks straying onward,
Sense with his dull eyes earthward bent,
  While Genius shot his glances sunward !

Away they go ! On roll the hours,
  And towards the west the day-god edges ;
See ! Genius holds a wreath of flowers,
  Fresh culled from all the neighboring hedges !
Alas ! ere eve their bright hues flit,
  While Common Sense (whom I so doat on !)
Thanked God "that he had little wit,"
  And drank his ketchup with his mutton.

THE TURQUOIS BROOCH.

They tell us of a precious stone
  Which changes with the wearer,
And, moved by sympathy alone,
  Grows lustreless or fairer.
Thus, if the loved one's bosom grieve,
  Its azure glory flies,
But if to joy that bosom heave,
  'Tis bright as summer skies.

So, Laura, is my soul to thee,
  By thee illumed or saddened,
O'ercast if thou look'st moodily,
  And bright if thou art gladdened.
Thus, like the turquois to my pain,
  Unlike to my unrest,
For, Laura, thou hast never ta'en
  My spirit to thy breast.

LINES

On reading in the Daily Times that "Louis Napoleon spends his evenings either playing backgammon with the Empress, or examining the private reports of the Chief of Police."

Spirit of him who drove afar
  Rebellion's hydra-headed brood,
And quenched the torch of civil war
  In tides of foreign blood!
Thou, in whose ears the dying groans
  Of old Tradition ever sounded!
Thou, at whose step the reeling thrones
  Of Europe fell, confounded!

Spirit of him, whose mind did forge
  At once the weapon and the chain—
The prince of princes, and the scourge
  Of all who were too weak to reign;
Behold this jackal of renown,
  Who from your name its glory snatches!
This mannikin beneath your crown,—
  This "king of shreds and patches!"

France weeps beneath the idiot sway
   Of shaveling priests and jeweled fools;
The cross of honor is the pay
   For Tyranny's most abject tools.
The land that couched the freest lance
   Now fears the informer's sightless arrow;
The eagle of imperial France
   Has dwindled to a sparrow!

And he, who staggered to a throne
   Through broken oaths and civic broil,
Who sought his perjury to atone
   By drenching red the Roman soil;
This dwarf, tricked out with seven-league boots,
   This king of thimble-rigging science—
This rat who gnaws the hoarded fruits,
   Designed to foster lions:

This perjurer, robber, murderer, all,
   Religion's curse and manhood's jibe,
Whose only battle is a ball,
   Whose only victory is a bribe—
This rushlight that would be a star
   (O Jupiter! immortal Ammon!)
Foregoes the glorious game of war
   For one of mild backgammon.

His bulletins, police reports,
  His aide-de-camp, the mousing spy—
Falsehood the passport to his courts,
  His life one long-continued lie;
And this was all the First did win,
  By Titan toil and daily battles;
And such "the pea that now within
  The giant's helmet rattles!"

A MAINE-LAW LYRIC.

With thickest growth of beard his face
  Was matted in a ghastly smile;
His hat preserved the faintest trace
  Of what was once a shapely tile;
His elbows glimmered through his coat,
  His trowsers needed tailor's care,
  His boots they were not of a pair,
And through them you his toes might note.
    He only said, "It is the tipple,
      The tipple 'tis," he said;
    He murmured, "Go it like a cripple,
      And go it 'till you 're dead!"

He raised his hand at dewy morn,
He raised it far into the night,
And, in a tone of maudling scorn,
The temperance party he would slight.
He drank his glass and called for more,
With trembling fingers searching out
For dimes within the tattered clout,
Which once the name of pocket bore.
He only said, " It is the tipple,
The tipple 'tis," he said;
He murmured, " Go it like a cripple,
And go it 'till you 're dead !"

Oft in the middle of the night
The wandering " star " his body found,
Stretched in the kennel, beastly " tight,"
And senseless in a trance profound;
He was a dweller in the Tombs
And from that prison when exempt,
He sought relief from self-contempt,
In brandy's soul-confusing fumes.
He only said, " It is the tipple,
The tipple 'tis," he said;
He murmured, " Go it like a cripple,
And go it 'till you 're dead !"

And ever as the lamp grew dim,
  And brandy lay beyond his reach,
He saw pale spectres glare at him,
  And mutter fiercely each to each.
O, they were hours to freeze the soul,
  When those blue corpses o'er him bent—
  And, to convey the moral meant,
Each fiend upheld a glittering bowl.
    He only said, "It is the tipple,
      The tipple 'tis," he said;
    He murmured, "Go it like a cripple,
      And go it 'till you 're dead!"

There is, within some granite walls,
  A high and hideous wooden thing,
And in its floor a door that falls,
  Obedient to a secret spring.
Aye; groan and shriek! With cries and tears,
  Mercy of earth and heaven demand;
  A wife's red blood is on your hand—
Your kindest gift to her for years!
    So ends the ballad of the tipple,
      Be warned, and pray and think;
    The tap is mother Murder's nipple,
      You suck blood as you drink!

A PALPABLE PARODY.

'Tis the last golden dollar,
Left shining alone;
All its brilliant companions
Are squandered and gone.
No coin of its mintage
Reflects back its hue—
They went in mint-juleps,
And this will go too!

I'll not keep thee, thou lone one,
Too long in suspense;
Thy brethren were melted,
And melt thou to pence!
I ask for no quarter,
I'll spend, and not spare,
Till my old tattered pocket
Lie centless and bare.

So soon may I follow
When friendships decay;
And from beggary's last dollar,
The dimes drop away!

When the Maine law has passed,
And the groggeries sink:
What use would be dollars,
With nothing to drink?

AN OLFACTORY ODE IN PRAISE OF NEW-YORK CLEANLINESS.

Thank Heaven! the crisis—
The terror is past,
And the sense they call smelling
Has perished at last;
And the anguish of smelling
Has perished at last.

Sadly I know
Of one sense I'm forlorn;
But, with pleasure and profit,
The loss may be borne;
With profit and pleasure
That loss may be borne.

And I walk so composedly
Now through the street,
That any beholder
Might fancy my feet
Were treading on roses,
All fragrant and sweet.

The stifling and choking,
The odors and stenches,
Are quieted now;
The olfactory wrenches,
That maddened my brow,
Are gone. Ah, those horrible,
Horrible stenches!

The sickness—the nausea—
The pitiless pain,
Have ceased with the smelling
That maddened my brain;
With the smell of the garbage
That rose to my brain.

And, oh! of all odors,
That odor the worst—
The odor commingled
Of cabbage accursed;

The odors of fish,
  And of cabbage accursed;
That torture no more
  In my nostril is nursed.

And, ah! let it never
  Be foolishly said,
That I am regretting
  The cold in my head;
The cold whence the numbness
  Of smelling is bred!

For now, all unheeding
  Olfactory wrenches,
I care not for Gotham—
  Its complicate stenches,
Its quintuple odors
  Of cumulent stenches—
Its fish, flesh and blood
  And its cabbage-stalk stenches.

And now I walk happily;
  Fearless of any
Diversified odors—
  Although there are many;
For my nostril is choked,
  And I care not for any.

And happy am I with
  A cold in my head!
The dank exhalation
  From garbage-heaps bred—
The sewerage and filth,
  Upon which hogs are fed—
Never trouble me, blest
  With a cold in my head.

RIME OF YE SEEDIE PRINTEERE MAN.

It is a seedie printeere man,
  And he stoppeth one of three—
" By thy unshorn beard and fevered eye
  Now wherefore stopp'st thou me?"

" For Jullien's band doth play to-night,
  And I must hence away;
The fiddles they are deftly tuned,
  Dost hear Herr Koenig play?"

He holds him with his grimy hand,
  "More copy!" he doth cry;
"Hold off, thou grisly printeere man!"
  The victim makes reply.

He holds him with his fevered eye,
  "More copy! it must come;
My printeeres they are standing still"—
  The editeere is dumb.

The editeere he sat him down,
  His teares they quickly ran,
While thus spake on the seedie one,
  The red-eyed printeere man:

"The papeeres must to-morrow out;
  To-morrow be on hand,
And you are our chief editeere—
  More copy we demand!"

"The Times comes out at early dawn,
  The Tribune follows soon,
The Mirror, Post, and the Express,
  They will be out by noon."
The editeere let fall a tear
  As he heard the loud bassoon.

Lo! Jullien to the daïs mounts,
A bearded wight is he;
With bugle-blow before him go
The merrie minstrelsy.

But still the steadfast printeere man
" More copy!" cries aloud—
Ye broken-hearted editeere
Withdraws him from the crowd.

" God save thee, wretched editeere!
What 'devils' plague thee thus?"
He ground an answer through his teeth—
It sounded like a cuss.

All night that wretched editeere
Before his desk did sit;
In vain for him had Mr. Brough
A free admission writ.

" More copy!" still the " devils" cry,
He cannot choose but make it;
And when his weary task is done,
He bids the " devil" take it!

Next morning when the sheet appeared,
  The public laughed amain;
They little thought the little jokes
  Had cost such mickle pain.

He wrote like one that had been dunned
  For copy, all forlorn;
A less harmonious Democrat
  He rose the morrow morn.

A TEMPERANCE PARODY.

I.

The grogshop stood open before me,
  Where late I had squandered my tin,
But I staggered, and something came o'er me,
  Which said it was vain to go in.
'Tis true I had spent my last quarter
  With friends—Tommy Sludge and Ned Dix:
But what are such "bricks" without mortar?
  And cash is the mortar of "bricks."

II.

I flew to the counter—the bar-maid
  Looked blue when I asked her to trust;
And I said, "Now (hic) don't be alarméd,
  I want (hic) to moisten my dust.
There lies (hic) the flask that can soften
  My pains, were I in (hic) death's jaws;
But why does the hand that (hic) often—
  Why now does that fair hand (hic) pause?"

III.

There was a time, falsest (hic) bar-maid,
  I loved you (hic) more than enough;
When the brandy, I thought, was (hic) charméd,
  Because you (hic) poured out the stuff.
But now, (hic) thou pimpled-faced daughter
  Of gin, (hic) how stained is thy glass!
And I'm—(hic) if I don't take to water,
  And vote (hic) the Maine law to pass.

IV.

Already the groggeries are reeling,
  The reign of the rum-fiend is o'er,
And law, a new feature revealing,
  Restrains where it punished before.

Then vote the Maine ticket we "oughter,"
  Preach, write for it—never be dumb;
On our side is virtue and water,
  On theirs is delirium and rum!

THE LOST CITY BROOM.

I.

Our tongues they were swollen and frothy;
  For the dust it was blinding and thick—
  The dust it was choking and thick;
And the hearts in our bosoms grew wrathy,
  And the blood in our pulses ran quick;
Our garments were dusted and mothy,
  As if they were powdered with brick—
And with garments all dusted and mothy
  It is hard to appear "like a brick!"

II.

Here once, in a coat of the newest,
  And pants inexpressive I walked—
  In pants that did shine as I walked.

They were days when my tailor was truest,
  And heard all the vows that I talked;
  All the vows that I recklessly talked:
And still when my prospects were bluest,
  To give me long tick, he ne'er balked—
Though my prospects were bankrupt and bluest,
  That tailor at tick never balked.

III.

Our fancies were noosed in a lasso,
  Our fancies were strangled and slain,
  Dirt-stifled, and throttled, and slain;
And we cried, both in tenor and basso,
  For gravel, for dust-cart's and rain—
  (Ah! globules of exquisite rain!)
We knew not the fair street of Nassau,
  (Though here we have lived and remain,)
Remembered not the good street of Nassau,
  In our thirst for the brow-cooling rain!

IV.

And now—while the whirling wind tosses
  The dust in the air like a fog—
  Like a foul and most palpable fog;
What vision my aching eye crosses,

And gives my dull fancy a jog—
A genial and generous jog?
An Alderman's ruby proboscis,
Begemmed with its blossoms of grog—
A flame-colored, fiery proboscis,
Distilled from quintessence of grog!

V.

And I said—"It is redder than copper;
It stands like a flame 'twixt his eyes—
'Twixt his cunning and black-beaded eyes:
He has seen that the dust is a stopper
On mouths that were uttering cries—
(Yea! anti-bad-Alderman cries!)
And he comes now to tell me a whopper,
A pack and a bundle of lies—
A bundle of infamous lies;
That, although like the flour from a hopper,
The dust from the dirty street flies,
Still he has done all that is proper
To save our unfortunate eyes!"

VI.

But the nose it burned redder and gayer.
That nose in my face he did thrust;
That flesh-case of rum he did thrust:

And he said, " Do you seek an allayer
  To conquer this delicate dust?
Do you, Oh unhappy tax-payer!
  Dislike to be smothered in dust?"
And he laughed, and his red nose grew gayer —
  He laughed 'till I thought he would burst,
While my hair stood on end and grew grayer,
  At the prospect of dying in dust—
  Of deplorably dying in dust!

VII.

I replied — " It is surely not pleasant;
  Not pleasant, as every one knows,
  As every bedusted one knows;
For the waste of Sahara, at present,
  O'er which the sirocco wind blows —
  (Raising billows of sand as it blows!)
That waste, now so anti-liquescent
  Has witnessed no dustfuller throes,
Than we, in square, alley, and crescent,
  In streets, and in lanes, and in rows,
Are called to endure, and look pleasant;
  But you — (ah! my God, how it glows!)
Come up from the City Hall crescent,
  With rum in your luminous nose!

VIII.

Thus I soothed the great man aldermanic,
  And tempted him out of his gloom —
  His fiery, sarcastical gloom;
And (though still his proboscis volcanic
  The dust-darkened air did illume,
And gleamed like the peak of Mount Yaanek —
  A rose of perpetual bloom !)
He led me along with titanic
  And muscular strength, 'till a tomb
Impeded his progress titanic —
  A dusty and legended tomb :
And I cried, " Will thine eyes aldermanic
  Declare what is writ on this tomb ?"
He replied —" 'Tis the broom ! 'tis the broom !
'Tis the grave of the lost city broom !"

IX.

Then my tongue it grew swollen and frothy,
  For the dust it was hideously thick —
  The dust it was stifling and thick ;
And the heart in my bosom grew wrathy,
  And the blood in my pulses ran quick—

The blood it leaped wildly and quick;
For the tomb it was dusted and mothy,
A tomb of derision-proof brick —
And with right arm, determined and wrathy,
I seized an immaculate stick —
A long, heavy, iron-shod stick;
But the copper-nose, flaccid and frothy,
Vamosed and evanished so quick,
That he felt not the weight of my stick —
Of my long, heavy, skull-cracking stick.

EPIGRAM.

[To a young lady who asked "The Letter H." for his name in her album.]

You ask for my name! ah, dear madam, you palter
With the hopes I have felt, as you well understand.
If you wish for my name, it is yours at the altar:
I'll give you my name when you give me your hand.

www.ingramcontent.com/pod-product-compliance
Lightning Source LLC
LaVergne TN
LVHW050526100826
845148LV00002B/455

* 9 7 8 1 4 2 5 5 1 9 9 0 2 *